GOD
Appointments

Fergus Buchan
with VAL WALDECK

GOD Appointments

Missionary Stories and Life Changing Meditations

with VAL WALDECK

Author of 'PLAY IT AS IT LIES'

Copyright

© GOD Appointments
Fergus Buchan

The right of *Fergus Buchan* to be identified as the author of the work has been asserted in accordance with the Copyright Act 98 of 1978.

All rights reserved.
No portion of this book may be reproduced in any form without written permission from the publisher or author, except as permitted by U.S. copyright law.

Compiled by:
Val Waldeck
email: vwaldeck@gmail.com

DTP:
Clive Thompson
International Professional Book Designer
https://www.getclive.com
Email: cliveleet1@gmail.com

Dedication

I dedicate this book to

Joanne,

my dear wife of 45 years.

You have been a pillar of strength and inspiration to me. Thank you for releasing me into the mission field these last 25 years, sometimes for months at a time, never complaining, just encouraging, and often coming with me.

My gratitude is eternal and unwavering.

Scripture

Scripture (unless otherwise indicated) is taken from the

New King James Version®.

Copyright © 1982 by Thomas Nelson. Used by permission. All rights reserved

Thank you to...

Jesus Christ
My Lord Jesus Christ Who died for me and gave me a second chance.

Joanne
My dear wife, Joanne, who has always stood by me, through the good times and the hard times.

My Children...
My children Fraser, Kirsty, Sheena, and Alistair (now with our Lord Jesus). What a blessing they have been to me.

To all...
All who have encouraged, supported, prayed for, travelled with, and stood by us over the years. There are so many names, it is impossible to mention all your names in this book but know that I love and appreciate every one of you. The Lord knows who you are, and your reward will come from Him.

Clive Thompson
Clive Thompson for the cover and layout design.

Val Waldeck
Val Waldeck for helping me capture these stories in book form.

Testimonials

Fergus, a fine Christian, lives his life as he preaches, a rare trait today. This book will inspire you to soar with Christ.
   Rob Mackenzie,
   MBE FRGS. Author of *David Livingstone, The Truth Behind the Legend.*

A man dedicated to serving our Lord. This is a man of God who lives by example, and what a great example he is to many without trying to be just that. He just is because He loves Jesus.
   Carl Erasmus,
   W.A. Australia.

If there is any minister of the Gospel who hears and listens to God before making any move or taking action, it is Dr Fergus. No wonder God led him to write a book on *God Appointments.* this is must-read. When God speaks it, so it shall be.
   Pastor Allan Menene,
   Wattvile, Johannesburg, South Africa.

I went to Karamoja, Northern Uganda with Fergus. While ministering under the trees to a local tribe, three witchdoctors arrived with bottles full of poison. They wanted to throw them at us, but angels miraculously kept them back.
   Johan Theron,
   Karoo, South Africa.

Dr. Fergus's uniqueness in preaching, with strong and encouraging messages and love to common Africans, influenced me a lot to be part of his mission outreaches.
   David Ssembuuze,
   Kampala Uganda.

I did a mission with Fergus to Zambia. I had just been retrenched but was committed to the mission and realised God has everything under control. It was one of the highlights of my life.
Eric Van Dyk,
Boksburg, South Africa.

Dr. Fergus's uniqueness in preaching, with strong and encouraging messages and love to common Africans, influenced me a lot to be part of his mission outreaches.
David Ssembuuze,
Kampala Uganda.

Leaving the 99 to find that one lost soul. That is Fergus. Missions...the Blessing and the cost.
Andrew Riddel,
Cape Town, South Africa.

It is my privilege to walk with Fergus. The righteousness in his heart shines in the beauty of his character.
Isabel Kruger,
Heilbronn, South Africa.

Fergus is a true servant of our lord Jesus Christ, with a Holy Spirit-led desire to fulfil Mark 16:15. He has travelled to wild and remote places to preach the gospel and fulfil his calling. He is a modern-day David Livingstone! Enjoy reading about his adventures!
Sean Caveney,
South Africa.

We have known Fergus for over thirteen years, a friendship which I believe was made in Heaven. Fergus and Joanne have stayed at our home many times. He attempted to teach us to hit a golf ball and it looked so easy when Fergus was standing next to us! Every time we pass a *Mugg &*

Bean, we have happy memories of Fergus and Joanne. We used to meet them for a *"brekkie"* and a chat whenever the opportunity arose. We also had a wonderful visit with them in London, a time we will never forget. I am so inspired and encouraged by Fergus. He truly is a Man of God and if we never meet again in the flesh because of all the chaos playing out in the world today, we will meet in heaven.
  Tommy & Priscilla Voget,
  South Africa.

It has been my privilege and joy to walk with Fergus and Joanne over the years. We have travelled and ministered together many times. It has been a privilege to help Fergus share these missionary stories and life-changing devotions with you.
  Val Waldeck,
  Author & Bible Teacher. www.valwaldeck.com.

Table of Contents

Dedication 5
Thank You to 6
Testimonials 7
Foreword 14
Preface 16

1. A Gift from God 19
2. A Large Harvest 21
3. A Serious Warning 24
4. A Time to Go 27
5. A Woman of Faith 30
6. African Hospitality 33
7. Ambassadors for Christ 35
8. Angus and I 37
9. Are You Willing to be a Missionary at Home? 39
10. Be Bold for Jesus 41
11. Be Strong in the Lord 43
12. Betrayed 45
13. Brotherly Love 48
14. C.T. Studd, Cricketer and Pioneer Missionary 51
15. Can God Use Your Worst Moments for His Glory? 54
16. Christmas 56
17. Commitment 58
18. Cul -De-Sacs 60

19.	David Livingstone, Missionary and Explorer	62
20.	Divine Appointments	65
21.	Doubt Weakens Faith	67
22.	Exercising Your Faith	70
23.	Expect Persecution In These End Times	73
24.	Expect to be Offended	75
25.	Faith in Action	77
26.	Given to Hospitality	79
27.	Giving Thanks	81
28.	God Can Melt The Hardest Heart	83
29.	God Has Your Back	85
30.	God is No Respecter of Persons	88
31.	God Wants You To Forgive, No Matter the Circumstances	90
32.	God's Protection	93
33.	Have You Felt Like Giving Up Lately?	95
34.	How to Handle Bribes	97
35.	I Was Blind But Now I See	99
36.	In Time of Trouble, Say	102
37.	Jesus Is Still The Healer	104
38.	Living In Unity	106
39.	Madame Guyon, a Life Transformed Through Prayer	108
40.	Making Wise Decisions	110
41.	Mean What You Say	112
42.	More About Prayer	114
43.	Moved by the Spirit	117
44.	My Vision of Alistair	119
45.	Never Despise Small Beginnings	121
46.	Never Judge a Book by its Cover	124

47.	No One Is Beyond the Reach of Jesus	127
48.	Patient in Tribulation	129
49.	Pilgrims Passing Through	131
50.	Practicing What We Preach	133
51.	Pray Always	135
52.	Put On the Whole Armour of God	137
53.	Ready In Season and Out of Season	139
54.	Righteous Anger	141
55.	Seasons In Our Lives	144
56.	Senders and Goers	146
57.	Servants on Assignment	149
58.	Stay In Your Lane	151
59.	Stefan and Theresa, Soldiers of the Cross	153
60.	Supplying and Essential Service	156
61.	Take Up Your Cross and Follow Jesus	158
62.	The Christian's Commission	160
63.	The Christmas Party	163
64.	The Desires of Your Heart	166
65.	The Faithfulness of God	169
66.	The God of the Impossible	171
67.	The Lord's Protection	173
68.	The Ministry of Angels	175
69.	The Power of the Blood of Jesus	178
70.	The Power of the Holy Spirit	181
71.	The Pygmies and Jesus	184
72.	The True Prosperity Gospel	187
73.	The Universal Gospel	189
74.	The Widow's Mite	192
75.	The Wind of the Spirit	194

76. The Power of the Blood 196
77. Trust in the Lord 199
78. What Has God Put In Your Heart? 201
79. When You Need Wisdom, Ask God 203
80. Whose Report Will You Believe? 205

About the Author 210
More Books by Fergus Buchan 212

Foreword

As Fergus' younger sister, I feel qualified to say I have known him all my life. From our days growing up in Zambia where he would relentlessly tease me, to supporting me through some challenging times in my life, he has always been a strong character, with determination and aspiration to meet any challenge head-on. Fergus' bravery and unquestioning faithfulness have inspired so many across the world.

Fergus's walk with the Lord has been traumatic in the extreme. Firstly, with the loss of his youngest son, Alastair, who was 4 years old at the time, and then his battle with cancer.

Having come to terms with the loss of Alastair and been reassured by the Lord that Alastair was safe and waiting for both him and Joanne, Fergus was able to continue his life as a golfer in Germany, serving the Lord as a strong Christian. Some years later, he was diagnosed with cancer and was given a prognosis of six to eight months to live. After real consideration, all treatment options with related outcomes were declined by both him and Joanne. Fergus put his healing in the Lord's hands. In his prayer he vowed, should the Lord choose to heal him, that he would serve the Lord for the rest of his life. This was over 20 years ago. I would like to confirm that Fergus has never received any treatment for cancer to date.

The Lord has led Fergus into many various and sometimes dangerous campaigns. He has never faltered or questioned the Lord's instructions. Fergus has relied only on the Lord's provision to carry out the work he has been charged to do. The verse that I feel describes my brother, whom I could not be prouder of, is:

Then I heard the voice of the Lord saying,
"Whom shall I send? And who will go for us?"
And I said,
"Here am I. Send me!"
Isaiah 6:8

May the Lord bless you and keep you on your travels and adventures.
Morag Collier

Preface

It is a pleasure and joy to serve the Lord. It has been my privilege to minister in many countries of the world, including South Africa, Australia, the United Kingdom, and the African Continent. My teams and I have ministered in many areas of Africa. We have been in KwaZulu-Natal in the Valley of a Thousand Hills with the Zulu people, where ancestral worship and the spirit world are very real. We have been in Zimbabwe (formerly Rhodesia), Zambia, Kenya with the Massai people, and further north in Uganda, war-torn Sudan, and the Central African Republic, where we led Pygmies to the Lord.

Many of the tribes I have spoken to walk around with spears, and bows and arrows. Some still practice human sacrifice. Most have never heard the Gospel. Many have not even heard the Name of Jesus Christ. The Lord has sent me to minister in the Sudanese refugee camps, preaching the Word of God in dangerous areas with the added danger of malaria, so rampant in Africa. Africa is a continent fraught with danger, disease, poverty, and war. I have been attacked and beaten by people who do not want to hear the Gospel, but the Great Commission spurs me on.

Jesus died to reconcile us to God. He became sin for us that in Him we might become righteous in Christ and prepared for Heaven. The Bible declares that whoever calls on the name of Jesus Christ will be saved, no matter who they are or where they live.

Jesus said, *"I must work the works of Him who sent Me while it is day; the night is coming when no one can work"* (John 9:4). We must work harder than ever while we have time. As George Whitfield said, let us rather wear out than rust out. Let us be busy in the marketplace, the highways and byways, the workplace, on the trains, in the football fields, in the schools, and wherever we find ourselves, making sure that people everywhere are given the opportunity to ensure their names are written in the *Lamb's Book of Life*.

By the Grace of God, we have reached thousands of men, women, and children for the Lord. Many of their stories are told in this book. My prayer is that you will be encouraged as you read and challenged to share the Good News in your sphere of influence.

Fergus Buchan
*Messiah Ministries International,
London, UK.*

GOD APPOINTMENTS

Fergus Buchan
with VAL WALDECK

1
A Gift from God

Who can find a virtuous wife? For her worth is far above rubies. The heart of her husband safely trusts her; So, he will have no lack of gain. She does him good and not evil All the days of her life,
Proverbs 31:10-12

This story is about Joanne and I travelling on the mission field. She wanted to come with me. And she did. One time, we travelled from Johannesburg to northern Kenya, a journey of about 5,000 kilometres. It took us about three-and-a-half weeks in a 4X4 Land Cruiser and trailer. We went through northern South Africa, right through Botswana, and crossed the Zambezi on a pontoon. It is now a bridge, but in those days, it was a pontoon – a flat-bottomed boat.

We drove through Zambia, crossed the border into Tanzania and continued travelling, camping, sleeping, and cooking out as we went. When we got to the bottom end of Kenya, in the Mombasa area, we ministered to many Muslims, which made some people in the area very unhappy.

Thereafter, we drove through the famous Rift Valley to northern Kenya. We stayed there for three months in our trailer and ministered right around the area. We went north, south, west, and east, and Joanne was by my side every step of the way.

I had one of the worst attacks of Malaria I have ever experienced during this time and was so grateful for Joanne. I came close to death, but she lovingly nursed me through it. Joanne did a lot of the driving, most of the cooking, and took care of everything. She set up the sound systems, the microphones, and generators. And she did all that while caring for me as well.

She is an absolute blessing to me. I don't know how many women would go through that without complaining and wanting to go home. Four countries… 5,000 kilometres… often sleeping in the bush because it wasn't safe to sleep on the side of the road, often facing danger from thieves, robbers, and unbelievers.

How many women would be prepared to stay home and look after the Home Front, releasing their husbands to fulfil their ministry and be away from home for months at a time? Joanne does.

Who can find a virtuous wife? I am so blessed because the Lord brought one into my life. Joanne is a Gift from God. We have travelled to many places together and shared everything. We have been married for 45 years and have four children. Fraser, Sheena, Kirsty, and little Alistair, now living with Jesus.

What a blessed man I am.

2
A Large Harvest

The harvest truly is plentiful, but the laborers are few.
Therefore, pray the Lord of the harvest to send out
laborers into His harvest.
Matthew 9:37-38

I don't know how many people there were on earth when Jesus spoke those words. But I do know there are more than 6 billion people living today. There are multitudes who need the Lord. We are so aware that the fields are ripe for harvest as we minister in the streets of London or in the rural areas of darkest Africa. The harvest is immense but sadly, the labourers are few.

Jesus had compassion and empathy for the lost, the sick, the weary, and the downtrodden in every walk of life. From the richest to the poorest, everyone needs the Lord. We must preach the Gospel and make disciples, no matter the circumstances.

How big is the harvest where you are living? Are you moved with compassion for them? The Bible speaks about people being like scattered sheep without shepherds. That is a good picture of our world today. Good shepherds are few and far between. There are some shepherds who have simply given up their ministry and walked away, leaving the sheep God called them to care for without hope. Churches have closed and become storerooms, playgrounds, and restaurants.

A great evangelist from the past, T.L. Osborne said a church that is not outward-looking and mission-oriented is a dead church. That is so true. We are not meant to just sit in church every Sunday, listen to the Word, and come back week after week. Yes, we need to meet and encourage one another, especially in these evil days. We need apostles, pastors, evangelists, teachers, and prophets to prepare us for works of ministry, but if we are not bringing in the lost, we are playing church. We were not born again to become pew sitters. We are called to share the Gospel, to go into the harvest fields and reap souls for Christ.

We are also called to petition the Lord of the harvest to send labourers into His harvest. How will they hear the Gospel if somebody doesn't go? Over the centuries, there have been men and women who left their comfortable lives of ease and set out to take the Gospel all over the world. Their life expectancy in Africa in the 1800's was often very short because of Malaria, Typhoid, Dysentery, wild animals, and tribesmen, but they went anyway. There are hundreds of unmarked graves in Africa of saints who have gone before us. They have a great reward because they went. I believe the highest call of God is to be a Missionary.

I want to challenge each reader to pick up your Bible, put your anointing oil in your bag, and go out and look for that lost sheep and lost coin in your local harvest field and in all the world, wherever the Lord leads you. The angels greatly rejoice when one sinner repents, and Heaven has a party.

Are you willing to be a labourer for God? If you can't go further afield than your local harvest, are you willing to pray for more labourers? Are you willing to support those labourers who give up everything to go? Professor Louw Alberts, an eminent South African scientist, made a thought-provoking statement at a Christian youth camp many years ago. He said, "Show me a man's chequebook, and I will tell you how committed that man is to the Lord Jesus Christ."

Are you willing to be an answer to your prayer for more labourers?

3
A Serious Warning

Now the Spirit expressly says that in latter times some will depart from the faith, giving heed to deceiving spirits and doctrines of demons
1 Timothy 4:1,2

It is a very serious thing to play with the occult. If you leave a window open, Satan will take advantage of that. He wants you to depart from the faith and be influenced by unbiblical teaching. Whole churches are turning from the Lord in these last days and following destructive heresies, *"having a form of godliness"* (2 Timothy 3:4) while denying the divinity of Christ Jesus, the inspiration of the Bible, and the true Gospel. The Bible says there are some untaught and unstable people who twist the scriptures, causing believers to fall away from the Truth (2 Peter 3:16,17).

We are told in the scriptures that evil spirits are looking for a place to inhabit. They want to possess human beings and turn them away from following the Lord Jesus Christ. Mark 5:11-16 records an incident in the Bible when the Lord commanded demons to leave a demon-possessed man. They look for somewhere to live and they entered a herd of pigs. We must avoid evil at all costs.

Believers, be careful what you watch on television and the

internet. Be cautious about what you read on social media and who you associate with. Do not go to palm readers, psychics, and witches. Avoid anything that glorifies and encourages witchcraft. Be very aware of the spirit world. It is very real. I have seen much of demonic activity in Africa, but it is going on in every part of the world. Every country is under attack.

If you have been involved in any form of demonic or spiritist activity, even certain exercises, repent today and return to the Lord. The prophet Isaiah challenged the people of Israel to walk in the light of the Lord. *"The Lord has rejected His people,"* he wrote, *"because they have filled their land with practices from the East, and with sorcerers, as the Philistines do. They have made alliances with pagans..."* (Isaiah 2:6 NLT).

Pray earnestly for loved ones who are being influenced and deceived by evil spirits.

I want to pray for anyone reading this who has opened a door or window to evil spirits. May you be delivered and set free as we pray together. I challenge you to get down on your knees right now and repent before the Lord.

Let us pray...
Father, I pray that every reader will understand the seriousness of what I'm sharing with them. Demonic activity is very real and very dangerous. Satan is still walking around like a roaring lion, seeking whom he may devour (1 Peter 5:8). Help my brothers and sisters to close doors, anoint their houses, and keep away from the occult, fortune tellers, palm readers, doctrines of demons, false teaching, and heresies. Lord, please keep them safe

from those who pervert and twist the scriptures. Deliver then as we pray together. I plead the Blood of the Lamb over them in the Name of the Father, the Son, and the Holy Spirit. Amen.

4
A Time to Go

To everything there is a season, A time for every purpose under heaven.
Ecclesiastes 3:1

After our season with Angus ended, and *Messiah Ministries International* was born, we sold our home and purchased the 72-hectare smallholding in Hermannsburg, KwaZulu-Natal. This was to be our Mission Station and home base.

Why would a professional Golfer want to take up farming? I didn't, but our plans were to have farm managers run the farming side, while Fraser and I travelled and evangelized. Unfortunately, these plans did not work out and we were left stranded when the two farmers working with us left suddenly. Joanne, Fraser, and Fikiswe, our faithful worker, looked at me and said, "What do we do now?" I told them, "We carry on with our vision."

It was a lot of hard work. We had cattle, 4,000 chickens, 10 acres of cabbage, and 10 hectares of maize. Fraser was able to travel more freely, but I had too much work to be able to leave the farm as much as I would have liked. Boundary fences and firebreaks had to be cut. Cattle and chickens needed to be cared for. Cabbages had to be taken to market. A 72-hectare farm is not easy to run alone.

I will never forget the day Keith Blond and Ethel van der Vyver came to help Joanne and me dip the cattle. First, we rounded them up in the back paddock. Then I ushered them in groups of three or four through a marrow run into the crush where Keith was waiting with the tick medicine. Joanne released them back into the paddock. Ethel stood by me with a pole, keeping the cows secure as they moved forward one by one. She lost focus for one moment and a cow kicked Ethel's pole so hard she went flying through the air like Mary Poppins. Fortunately, she was not hurt. We basically got the job done but we couldn't stop laughing.

My farming career was very short! But it took an incident with the chickens to finally convince me that this season was over. Jesus said, *"No one, having put his hand to the plough, and looking back, is fit for the kingdom of God"* (Luke 9:62). Well, I put my hand to that plough, I really tried my level best, but I knew in my heart it was the wrong plough I was holding onto so doggedly. I repented, and the Lord saw my heart and released me from farming a month later.

I will tell you the story about the chickens next and the lesson I learned about the importance of staying in your lane.

Sometimes, you have to let go of whatever you are doing in your attempts to fulfil your calling and allow the Lord to show you His Way. It may be your career, your ministry, your church, or your dream. It is very hard to move a stationary car. There are also times when you may want to go, but the Lord wants you to stay and finish the course. There is a season and a time for every purpose under heaven. Be sure not to miss your season.

Is God speaking to you?

5

A Woman of Faith

And He said to her, "Daughter, your faith has made you well. Go in peace, and be healed of your affliction."
Mark 5:34

Mark's Gospel tells us about a woman who had a flow of blood for twelve years and had suffered many things from many physicians. She had spent all that she had and was no better, but rather grew worse. We can relate to that. Many people have sold their homes and cars and gone bankrupt just to pay off medical debts. There seemed to be no hope for her.

Then she heard about Jesus. When He touched people, they were healed. She must have heard many testimonies from the people in her town and faith rose in her heart. Mere mental assent is not enough. What we believe must be mixed with faith. *"For indeed the gospel was preached to us as well as to them; but the word which they heard did not profit them, not being mixed with faith in those who heard it"* (Hebrews 4:2).

This woman acted on her faith. She came behind him in the crowd and touched his garment. She said, "If only I may touch his clothes, I shall be made well." That was an act of faith because touching a Rabbi in those days was taboo, especially as a woman and in her condition.

She was prepared to go public with her faith. She ignored the crowds and forced her way to Jesus. This humble woman made no demands. She didn't insist on being prayed for or having His hands touch her. She was determined just to touch the hem of His garment. Her faith was focused on Jesus. Mark 5:29 tells us what happened. *"Immediately the fountain of her blood was dried up, and she felt in her body that she was healed of the affliction."*

When the Holy Spirit comes upon you, you know something happened. You don't hope you were healed or talk yourself into believing it. You can't always explain or understand what happened. I couldn't explain it when the Holy Spirit came upon me as I was lying in the cancer ward. I just knew I was healed.

The Lord knows when people touch Him by faith and the Holy Spirit ministers to them. "And Jesus, immediately knowing in Himself that power had gone out of Him, turned around in the crowd and said, 'Who touched my clothes?'" The disciples said, *"You see the multitude thronging You, and you say, 'Who touched Me?"* (v.31). He knew who touched Him by faith. So why did He ask that question?

It is important to acknowledge and be thankful when the Lord answers our prayers. One day Jesus healed ten lepers and only one returned to thank Him. *"Didn't I heal ten men? Where are the other nine?"* (Luke 17:17-19). Giving thanks strengthens our faith and encourages others.

Humility and faith go hand-in-hand. She did not boast

about her faith or claim to be anyone special. She trembled as she bowed before Him and shared her story. *"And He said to her, 'Daughter, your faith has made you well. Go in peace, and be healed of your affliction"* (Mark 5:34).

"Faith sees the invisible, believes the unbelievable, and receives the impossible" Corrie Ten Boom.

6

African Hospitality

Be hospitable to one another without grumbling.
1 Peter 4:9

We were on a mission trip in Zimbabwe, heading towards the Victoria Falls. We were travelling in three cars and, if I remember correctly, there must have been eight people in our team, including Joanne and myself.

When we arrived in Livingstone, our host greeted us warmly. "Is this your team?" he asked as we watched the group getting out of the vehicles.

"Yup, that's us," I said. "We have arrived."

"Uh," said our host, "Where are you sleeping?"

We didn't have caravans or tents in those early days and assumed our host would take care of those details.

"Don't worry," I said, "We will make a plan. We will find a Bed & Breakfast somewhere."

"No, no," he said anxiously. "You are our guests and I think I have a place for you. Wait here."

He was gone for about an hour. "Follow me," he said when he returned.

We followed him into a township, and he stopped outside a completed brick home. "I'll show you where you are going to sleep," he said. "But, first, let me introduce you to the owner."

We went into the house with him, and he introduced us to a delightful African woman. "You are welcome, Man of God," she said warmly. "This is going to be your home while you and your team are ministering here."

"But this is your house," I protested. "Where are you going to stay?"

"I know its my house," she smiled. "I am going to stay with my sister. My family are also moving out. Everything is prepared for you. All the beds are made, the kitchen is clean, and there is hot water for your bath."

We stayed there for about four days, and it was very comfortable. Clean as a whistle and everything we needed in place. That Zimbabwean woman also made a huge pot of mielie meal for our supper, complete with cabbage and pieces of chicken. After that we looked after ourselves because she couldn't afford to feed us, nor did we expect her to.

I will never forget the hospitality of that Zimbabwean lady. It is something white people can learn from our African brethren. Their hospitality is amazing.

"Cheerfully share your home with those who need a meal or a place to stay" (1 Peter 4:9 NLT).

The Bible encourages us to be hospitable to one another without grumbling.

7
Ambassadors for Christ

Now then, we are ambassadors for Christ, as though God were pleading through us: we implore you on Christ's behalf, be reconciled to God.
2 Corinthians 5:20

Many years ago, I was ministering in Zambia. I happened to be back in my old hometown where Angus and I grew up. I was a pupil of Kitwe Boy's High School in Zambia where I received the international cricket cap as a schoolboy. I was also a prefect, not because of my academic studies, but because of my sporting abilities, I think.

I remember the day the headmaster called the prefects and asked us to round up the whole school as a special guest was to speak to them. It was a big school with about 1000 students and we soon got them lined up. The speaker was an American Negro, Jesse Owens, and he encouraged us to never give up working hard as we pursued our goals. It was very inspirational and motivating.

Afterwards, I discovered that Jesse Owens was the first man ever to win four medals at the 1936 Olympic Games in Munich, Germany, during Hitler's time. They refused to give him any medals simply because he was a black man. This godly man returned to America and was shunned again because of his skin colour. The victorious American

Olympic team was invited to the White House for tea, except for Jesse Owens. What strikes me as I look back to my school days, is that there was never any hint of malice, hatred, or bitterness about his past experiences when Jesse Owens spoke to us. What an example he set.

I visited my old school while I was in the area and asked the headmaster if I might address the school. He was happy for me to do so and gathered all the schoolboys in the assembly hall. They gave me a warm welcome and resounding applause. I was the only old boy, and certainly the only White old boy to come back and speak to them.

I came as the Ambassador of Christ and 700 young men gave their life to Christ that day. It was a great honour and privilege for me and a highlight of my life. I didn't return to share my sporting achievements but came with the gospel of Jesus Christ.

May we have the same heart as the Apostle Paul. He wrote, *"For I determined not to know anything among you except Jesus Christ and Him crucified"* (1 Corinthians 2:2).

8
Angus and I

Who then is Paul, and who is Apollos, but ministers through whom you believed, as the Lord gave to each one? I planted, Apollos watered but God gave the increase. So then neither he who plants is anything, nor he who waters, bur God who gives the increase. Now he who plants and he who waters are one, and each one will receive his own reward according to his own labor.
1 Corinthians 3:5-8

Angus and I both have one vision, to reach the lost in response to Jesus' last recorded words found in Matthew 28:18-20. *"And Jesus came and spoke to them, saying, 'All authority has been given to Me in heaven and on earth. Go therefore and make disciples of all the nations, baptizing them in the name of the Father and of the Son, and of the Holy Spirit, teaching them to observe all things that I have commanded you; and lo, I am with you always even to the end of the age.' Amen"*

When I came back from Germany, I joined my brother Angus' ministry. We worked closely together for five years at *Shalom Ministries* in Greytown, South Africa. Our vision remained the same, but our goals changed. Angus, carried on with the ministry the Lord gave him, which included major outreaches to men and online ministry. Joanne and I felt called, together with our son, Fraser, to reach the less travelled areas of the world.

And so, *Messiah Ministries* was born.

Angus and I keep in close touch, we pray together and love one another dearly. But we are working in different fields, reaching the lost in different ways. Fraser and his wife, Marta, are now serving the Lord in America. None of us are more important than the other. We are watering and planting, but God is giving the increase.

The heart of *Messiah Ministries* is to seek the lost coin and the lost sheep in the streets of London, and especially in the most remote areas of the world. Most are difficult places to reach where few missionaries can go, including the huge refugee camps in places like the Sudan and Rwanda. This is the ministry to which the Lord has called us. Very often, we do not have formal meetings, but walk into remote areas and find individuals or groups of people who need to hear about Jesus. "For if I preach the gospel I have nothing to boast of for necessity is laid upon me; yes, woe is me if I do not preach the gospel" (1 Corinthians 9:16).

Do you feel like that? I challenge you to pray, "Lead me to some soul today, and teach me, Lord, just what to say?"

9

Are You Willing to be a Missionary at Home?

And Jesus came and spoke to them, saying, "All authority has been given to Me in heaven and on earth. Go [therefore and make disciples of all the nations, baptizing them in the name of the Father and of the Son and of the Holy Spirit, teaching them to observe all things that I have commanded you; and lo, I am with you always, even to the end of the age". Amen.
Matthew 28:19,20

Messiah Ministries International has its headquarters in London now. We work as missionaries in Central Africa and on the streets of London. Every week, we walk the streets looking for the lost and telling them about Jesus. We are a mission in the heart of London and a small church in Fulham where we disciple believers.

Not everyone is called to be a Missionary in rural areas, but everyone is called to be a missionary in the Mission Field where you live every day… in your home, your city, your office, wherever you find yourself.

"But you will receive power and ability when the Holy Spirit comes upon you; and you will be My witnesses [to tell people about Me] both in Jerusalem and in all Judea, and Samaria, and even to the ends of the earth" (Acts 1:8 Amplified Bible).

You can have a mission in Beijing, Johannesburg, Paris, or anywhere you live. You don't have to go to the far-flung continents of Africa or Mongolia. David Wilkerson came to New York City as a Missionary. We must go where the Lord leads us.

I'm led to go to the lost and especially where people haven't had a chance to hear the gospel. Where we go, we must take generators, our own lighting, and our own food because the people we go to can barely feed themselves. There is no greater privilege or greater honour than seeing people bend their knees and give their lives to Jesus Christ. What greater gift can one give to anyone other than introducing them to Jesus and securing their eternal future?

Are you seeking to make a name for yourself? Desiring to plant a big ministry? Striving to live a prosperous lifestyle? Is the Lord Jesus Christ your focus?

Who we are is not important. In Central Africa, the villagers don't even know my name. They refer to me in their language as that white man with the big hat. They don't know the name of our ministry. All they know is that we brought them the Word of God and people's lives were changed. People were born-again and some were healed. Villages changed, and the drinking stopped. Jesus Christ, Son of God, made a difference in their community.

Where is the Lord leading you to share the Gospel? Who has He laid on your heart?

10
Be Bold for Jesus

And they went out and preached everywhere, the Lord working with them and confirming the Word through the accompanying signs. Amen.
Mark 16:20

I have ministered in many countries of the world but am primarily called to minister in Africa. Over the past twenty years, this ministry has reached many thousands of people in unreached areas. Missionary work is very relevant in this day and age. There are still many unreached people who have never heard the Name of Jesus.

Some folks have experienced a touch of missions, but if you really want to experience missionary work in the raw, you should come with us. We don't fly into cities and stay in Holiday Inns, enjoying three-day conferences in air-conditioned rooms. Our teams often consist of only three or four people. We sleep rough and eat whatever is available. We minister under trees usually, and sometimes by candlelight in straw huts.

I understand that this type of mission work is not for everybody. It is a setup fraught with pitfalls, danger, disease, and disappointments. The food is basic and sometimes there is no food. Mission work is not easy. You stand a good chance of being beaten and attacked by people who do not want to hear the gospel. Nevertheless, we must fulfil the Great Commission. Mission work may not be comfortable, but the joy of seeing people respond to the Gospel is very exciting.

We were in Karamoja, Northern Uganda in 2019. The local tribe consisted of about three hundred people, and they all came to hear us share the gospel. It was a very rural area. The Elders and Chiefs sat under a tree at a distance on my right, looking at me with suspicion. I believe the Lord Jesus came to share the gospel and heal the sick, so that is our mission too. We always pray for the sick and trust the Lord to confirm His Word through signs following the ministry.

This day there was a young girl in the crowd. She was suffering from epilepsy. She seemed to be in a trance. She was shaking badly and kept falling over, lying on the ground with her tongue protruding out of her mouth. I walked over to this young girl, praying as I laid hands on her. The people and their leaders watched silently.

The next day, the tribe was astonished to see her joyfully dancing in front of them. They listened intently as his young girl gave her testimony in her own language. She was completely healed. There were no more fits. The Chiefs and Elders knelt in the dust and gave their lives to Jesus. "This man's God that he preaches about," they said, "is far more powerful than our gods."

You may not be called to rural mission work, but there are many unreached people in your city and suburb. Why not step out for Jesus and tell them about the Saviour? Open yourself to the ministry of the Holy Spirit so the Gifts of the Spirit may confirm your word with signs following.

Will you take up the challenge to be bold for Jesus?

11

Be Strong in the Lord

"Finally, my brethren, be strong in the Lord and in the power of His might. Put on the whole armor of God, that you may be able to stand against the wiles of the devil.
Ephesians 10:10,11

I have walked with the Lord Jesus Christ for many years and have come to know that the devil is a bully. He comes against the children of God in every way he can. He's a master at stirring up fear and unbelief and knows how to make trouble. He's been doing this for a very long time. He comes against our families, health, finances, business, and relationships. We are living in the Last Days and the devil knows his time is short. Be sure, he will come at us with all he's got and turn up the heat.

The Bible says we must resist him in the power of the Lord. That is the only way to handle bullies. *"Therefore submit to God. Resist the devil and he will flee from you"* (James 4:7). Why will he flee? The Word says, *"... because He who is in you is greater than he who is in the world"* (1 John 4:4). If we are walking closely with the Lord, we can take whatever comes our way in His strength. Make a firm decision to be strong in the Lord. Don't give an inch, dig your heels in, no matter what comes your way. If you know the Lord Jesus Christ and you are filled with the Holy Spirit, you can face anything.

We have been in dangerous places on the mission field. Our teams have faced hardship, terrorists, demon-possessed people, and much more. The Lord has always been true to His Word and given us the strength to stand firm and keep going.

Of course, we must do our part. *"Therefore, put on every piece of God's armor so you will be able to resist the enemy in the time of evil. Then after the battle you will still be standing firm. Stand your ground, putting on the belt of truth and the body armor of God's righteousness. For shoes, put on the peace that comes from the Good News so that you will be fully prepared. In addition to all of these, hold up the shield of faith to stop the fiery arrows of the devil. Put on salvation as your helmet, and take the sword of the Spirit, which is the Word of God. Pray in the Spirit at all times and on every occasion. Stay alert and be persistent in your prayers for all believers everywhere."*
Ephesians 10:11-18 (NLT).

Pray about everything. Pray for one another. Pray for your family. Break bread regularly. Plead the Blood of the Lamb over your family, your friends, your church, your relationships, and your business. Read the Bible daily and spend time with the Lord and His people.

12

Betrayed

Then Peter, turning around, saw the disciple whom Jesus loved following, who also had leaned on His breast at the supper, and said, "Lord, who is the one who betrays You?"
John 21:20

Jesus' group of disciples worked together as a team. They travelled together, ministered together, and shared their lives. Who could have imagined one of them would

We were on our way home after an extremely exciting and dangerous mission into the Congo basin. When we arrived at the Congo border, we could see David waiting for us on the other side of no man's land. There were four of us in the car, myself, our lady interpreter, a Bishop I have worked with for many years and trusted implicitly, and a friend.

We got out of the vehicle to go to the immigration office. But I sensed there was a problem. A group of four men were looking at us and I could see trouble ahead. I had no idea what was going on, but I knew it was not good.

"Pastor," my interpreter said, "We've got a problem here. These men are expecting the payment for the rental of the 4X4 vehicle you hired to go into the jungle."

"It has been paid," I said. "Ask the Bishop. I sent him the money long ago."

Everybody looked at the Bishop, but he just walked away. It turned out he had spent the money and never paid the bill.

"We had better pray, Pastor," she said. "These are Congolese men. I heard them speaking to one another. They are going to shoot you."

I called on the Lord with everything I had. I knew it was not an idle threat. They were serious.

The leader walked across to me and said through my interpreter, "Where's our money?"

"I thought you had been paid," I responded, trying to explain the situation. "I don't have any money on me."

"That doesn't help us," he shouted. "I don't care if it's him. You are the one responsible to pay."

They looked at each other and I could see their weapons under their coats. We had reached a crisis point.

"Lord," I prayed, "You have got to help me now."

I looked the leader in the eye and said, "Sir, I am a man of God. I've never broken my word. I will send you the money via Western Union tomorrow morning when we reach Kampala."

My interpreter interrupted, "You can trust this Pastor," "Why should I?", he growled, "When he goes across tha t border, how do I know he will keep his word?"

"You can trust me," I said firmly. "Just give me your bank details and you will have the money in the morning."

The four men had a heated discussion before the leader returned. "All right," he said, "We will trust you."

What a relief it was to go through immigration and walk across no man's land to David and our transport home. The Bishop said nothing the whole while. He kept his distance behind us. The last straw was when the interpreter said she hadn't been paid either and didn't have enough money for a visa to return to Uganda. I gave her my last $50.

I was livid. We had a long drive home. Nobody said a word. The next morning, I sent the money as promised. The Bishop began apologising profusely and promising to pay the money back. It was a large sum of money, but to this day we have never received it. Betrayal at the hands of someone you trust cuts deep, but I have forgiven him. It was a serious situation, but the Lord Jesus Christ stood by us.

The Lord Jesus is a Friend who will never betray you. Keep your eyes on Him at all costs.

13

Brotherly Love

Let brotherly love continue.
Hebrews 13:1 NKJV

Let love of your fellow believers continue.
Hebrews 13:1 Amplified Bible

I was on my way to the Congo on our mission to reach the Pygmies. Boarding at Heathrow airport, I was delighted to be assigned a seat with lots of leg room and two empty seats in my row. "Oh great," I thought. "I've got all three seats to myself. I can stretch out later."

We flew to Rwanda. After a twenty-minute wait on the plane, I was getting ready to settle down for the last leg of my journey when I looked up to see a huge man coming down the aisle. He was the biggest man I have ever seen. He had to bend over to get into our part of the cabin. This African American, wearing a hoodie, was 6 foot 10 at least. And, would you believe it, he sat down on my aisle seat, my anticipated sleeping space! We looked at each other and nodded a greeting as we took off for Rwanda

"Good day, Sir," he said, introducing himself as George Blakeney.

I greeted him and we began chatting.

"Where are you going?" he asked.

"I'm going to Uganda. Then driving into the Congo basin."

"Why are you going to the Congo?"

"I'm a missionary and I am going to look for a tribe of Pygmies to bring them the Word of God. That's what I do. So, what do you do?"

George told me he was an NBA basketball player from North Carolina. I smiled when I thought about just meeting the largest man I've ever known while on my way to find the smallest people in the world.

"Are you a Christian?" I asked.

"Yes, Sir, I am born again," he said with a big smile.

That day we struck up a friendship that has lasted the test of time. We couldn't stop talking about the Lord Jesus and enjoyed wonderful fellowship. This was a genuine case of brotherly love.

"Do you want to break bread with me?" I asked later.

"That would be crazy," he responded enthusiastically.

We used a bread roll and some Coco-Cola as we shared Communion. It was a very special moment for both of us.

When we landed at Rwanda, George disembarked. "God bless you," he said. "I hope you do well. I will be in touch with you."

He bent down to go through the archway to the exit.

Suddenly, he stopped and pointed his finger at me. "I will see you again," he said, and he was gone.

True to his words, George has kept in close touch. We pray together weekly, and George also regularly attends our online *Messiah Ministries International* prayer meetings on Wednesday evenings. He's planning to visit us in London. The friendship we developed on that aircraft was God-ordained. It has brought George into a wider circle of Christian friends and enriched all our lives.

These are the kind of friendships we must invest in. Trust the Lord for some God-ordained friends that will add value to your life and theirs.

"Let love of your fellow believers continue. Do not neglect to extend hospitality to strangers [especially among the family of believers – being friendly, cordial, and gracious, sharing the comforts of your home and doing your part generously], for by this some have entertained angels without knowing it" (Hebrews 13:1,2 Amplified Bible).

14

C.T. Studd, Cricketer and Pioneer Missionary

And I, brethren, when I came to you, did not come with excellence of speech or of wisdom declaring to you the testimony of God. For I determined not to know anything among you except Jesus Christ and Him crucified.
1 Corinthians 2:1

C.T. Studd was a famous British cricketer in the late 1800's. He was the youngest of three sons born into a very wealthy family in England. The three brothers all played cricket, but C.T. Studd was considered England's most outstanding cricket player. The Men's Ashes is a Test cricket series played biennially between England and Australia and its symbol of victory is a small urn containing the ashes of a cricket bail. C.T. Studd's name is engraved on that urn.

While C.T. Studd was studying at Cambridge University, something happened that changed his life forever. A famous missionary from Chicago in the USA came to town. D.L. Moody was an uneducated man by worldly standards who had a poor grasp of the English language. He couldn't read or write until the age of thirteen, but when he found the Lord, Moody was unstoppable as an evangelist.

D.L. Moody was invited to speak to the students at the prestigious Cambridge University. C.T. Studd and six other Cambridge students (known as the Cambridge Seven), dedicated their lives to foreign missionary service. The wealthy student gave away his entire fortune in one night. "Some wish to live within the sound of Church or Chapel bell," he wrote. "I want to run a Rescue Shop within a yard of hell."

C.T. Studd ministered in China, India, and Africa, and planted over 600 churches. He loved Africa and spent most of his time in the Congo, where he passed away in 1930 at the age of 70. One of his famous sayings was "Only one life, 'twill soon be past; Only what's done for Christ will last." His last recorded utterance as he passed into eternity was *"Hallelujah!"*

C.T. Studd was passionate about the *Great Commission*. This was his challenge to Christians:

"Christ's call is to feed the hungry, not the full; to save the lost, not the stiff-necked; not to call the scoffers, but sinners to repentance; not to build and furnish comfortable chapels, churches, and cathedrals at home in which to rock Christian professors to sleep by means of clever essays, stereotyped prayers and artistic musical performances; but to raise living churches of souls among the destitute; to capture men from the devil's clutches and snatch them from the very jaws of hell; to enlist and train them for Jesus, and make them into an Almighty Army of God. But this can only be accomplished by a red-hot, unconventional, unfettered Holy Ghost religion, where neither Church nor State, neither man nor traditions are worshipped or preached, but only Christ and Him crucified." [*The Intercessor, Vol 26 No 1*/Excerpt from *Summit Living*, by Stewart Dinnen].

"The world has yet to see what God can do with a man fully consecrated to him. By God's help, I aim to be that man." – D.L. Moody.

That was C.T. Studd's heart too, and it is mine.

How about you?

15

Can God Use Your Worst Moments for His Glory?

And we know that all things work together for good to those who love God, to those who are the called according to His purpose.
Romans 8:28

The death of our little four-year-old son, Alistair, changed the course of our lives forever. Joanne and I are living testimonies of the truth of Romans 8:28. God can use your worst moments for His Glory.

We were visiting my brother, Angus Buchan, on his farm in Greytown, South Africa. It was Jill's birthday, and we were all outside playing cricket. Alistair came running up to me. "Daddy," he said excitedly, "can I go with Aunty Angus on the tractor?" He loved his uncle and always called him Aunty Angus. "Ask your mom," I said and off he ran. I never dreamed it would be the last time I spoke to Alistair. About fifteen minutes later one of Angus' staff came running into the yard. "There's been an accident," he shouted. "You must go to the hospital immediately."

My career and money meant nothing now as I held the broken body of my little son and ran my fingers through his blond hair. Joanne and I felt as though our hearts had been ripped out of our chests as we made our way back to the farm. Could anything good come out of this?

I didn't know what to do with myself. I walked out into the maize fields. A storm was brewing. I fell on my knees, weeping in the pouring rain. That day I surrendered my life completely to Jesus Christ. I don't know how long I stayed out there but I knew I had an encounter with God.

It took time to go through the process of grieving, but God brought us out of the deepest, blackest hole we have ever been in our lives. It wasn't easy but God knows how to bring glory out of tragedy.

The passing of Alistair has made an enormous impact on the lives of those who have heard our story. This tragedy resulted in my call to become a missionary and lead hundreds of thousands to the Lord throughout Africa and beyond. *Messiah Ministries International* is a missionary ministry. Our base is in London and our goal is to make disciples of those we reach on the streets of London. Our vision is to take the Gospel to places where few ministries go. Our heart is for the lost and the needy, the outcasts, the poorest of the poor, especially in the rural areas of Africa. We aim to do what Jesus did – preach the Gospel and heal the sick.

Losing a loved one, and especially a child, is probably one of the hardest things to go through. Keep your eyes on Jesus no matter what is happening in your life. You can trust God to bring you through your trial. He knows how to work everything together for the good of those who love Him.

16

Christmas

I have become all things to all men, that I might by all means save some. Now this I do for the gospel's sake, that I may be partaker of it with you.
1 Corinthians 9:22,23

I love Christmas. It is a wonderful family time. Above all, it is a time when we celebrate the advent of the Lord Jesus Christ. It is an excellent opportunity to share the Gospel as we remind people about the reason Christ came the first time and challenge them to prepare their hearts for His prophesied return. He came as a Babe to pay the price for our sins. When He returns, it will be as the Judge of all the earth (John 5:22,23). Every eye will see Him, every knee will bow, and every tongue will confess Him as King of kings and Lord of lords.

Some Christians insist that Christmas is a pagan festival and choose to ignore this glorious Gospel opportunity. You will remember that Christianity was banned in the first three centuries and Christians used the pagan holiday festivals as an opportunity to celebrate Jesus and share the Gospel. We can do the same. Give someone a tract and they may throw it away. Give them a beautiful Christmas card with the Gospel message and they read every word.

A Pastor friend of mine in South Africa lives in a very

big Muslim community. He makes full use of this gospel opportunity. Every year, he puts the biggest Christmas tree he can find outside his house, decorated to the hilt. Everybody who comes to his home comments on the tree, and it gives him the opening to talk about Jesus.

I was preaching in Soweto, near Johannesburg in a massive tent. It was a very dangerous area with a history of drugs, alcohol, and gangs. As people responded to the altar call, one young man ran down the middle of the aisle. He was in his early twenties. He dived onto the platform, skidded about three meters, and fell onto his knees, crying out to Jesus for mercy. He was saved and delivered in an instant as the Lord Jesus touched him. The gospel of Christ *"is the power of God to salvation for everyone who believes, for the Jew first and also for the Greek"* (Romans 1:16).

In season and out of season, use every opportunity the Lord gives you to share the Gospel with your generation. Celebrate the Christ of Christmas. Point people to the Cross and His Resurrection at Easter. "Avoid foolish disputes, genealogies, contentions, and strivings about the law; for they are unprofitable and useless" (Titus 3:9). The times are urgent. *"I must work the works of Him who sent Me while it is day; the night is coming when no one can work"* (John 9:4).

17

Commitment

But Jesus said to him, "No one, having put his hand to the plow, and looking back, is fit for the kingdom of God."
Luke 9:62

We were in northern Kenya. It was the final week of our crusade, and I was due to preach at a local church on the following Sunday. On Monday morning, prior to the Sunday meeting, I woke up feeling hot, then cold, shivering and shaky. Joanne was worried that I had Malaria again. She prayed over me and gave me some painkillers.

The next morning, I was worse. Local pastors came to pray for me and one of them took me to a doctor. He confirmed I had Malaria. He said, "Take these three tablets, some painkillers, and drink lots of fluids. You should feel better in the morning."

Wednesday morning, I was worse. I had a very bad strain of Malaria. An elderly doctor in his eighties saw me this time. "Tell your husband he is going to die if he doesn't go to hospital," he said to Joanne when I refused.

Finally, he agreed to give me some medication. He injected me with insulin. He handed Joanne more insulin and instructed her to take me to the local mission hospital every day at the same time for more injections. We went back to our caravan, and I lay on a stretcher in the tent. I couldn't sit or stand. I was very weak.

After the second injection. I must have gone into a coma. I was aware of the Pastors praying for me and Joanne standing on my righthand side. A blackness came over me and I felt myself slipping away. I had total peace. But it was not my time, and I awoke late in the afternoon. Someone brought fresh orange juice and it was the only thing that stayed down in nearly four days.

Sunday arrived and I made it to the meeting. There were approximately 300 people there. Many had walked miles to be present. In Africa, you don't preach for twenty minutes. They expect at least two to three hours. Halfway through my sermon, it was time for the next injection. The hospital was about three kilometres away. When we arrived, those humble people allowed me to go to the front of the long queue. They have such respect for those who bring the Word of God.

Two things stand out for me. One was the commitment of those precious people. No one left the service while we went to the hospital. They sang and praised the Lord while they waited. They were hungry for the Word of God.

The other was a young man who noticed the wind blowing the pages of my Bible as I preached. He stood next to me and held the pages firm, keeping his finger on the scriptures I was reading. Every time I looked at my Bible, I knew exactly where to read next. When we got back, his finger was still on the last scripture I had read. "That's where you finished," he said. That is commitment.

May I challenge you to be committed to your church or fellowship? Support your pastor, listen to the sermons carefully and think about what you hear. Be faithful in attendance and service.

18
Cul-De-Sacs

...lest satan should take advantage of us; for we are not ignorant of his devices.
2 Corinthians 2:11

A *cul-de-sac* is a route or course, a dead end, leading nowhere. The devil is a master at distracting and diverting us from advancing the gospel. He will always try and find a way to stop us and lead us into *cul-de-sacs*. He looks for our weak spots, picks on our families, and attacks our health. The Bible says we must always *"Put on the whole armor of God, that you may be able to stand against the wiles of the devil"* (Ephesians 6:11). We must not be ignorant of his devices.

Years ago, when we were operating from our Mission Station in Hermannsburg, KwaZulu-Natal, Fraser and I went to Zimbabwe on a mission trip. We planned to be away for about a week and left Joanne and a friend, Ethel van der Vyver, at home. One evening they were closing the church and outhouses when they heard the dogs barking. Joanne saw a shadow in the dark and realised burglars were in the yard. The police failed to arrive, but German neighbours answered her call and rushed to their aid. They were heavily armed, and the burglars fled.

The next night, the burglars came back. This time they managed to steal quite a lot of equipment before the Germans arrived and put them to flight again. Our staff were there during the day. And those wonderful neighbours organised security to watch over Joanne and Ethel at night.

Of course, Fraser and I were highly upset and wanted to come home immediately. My brave wife insisted we continue with the planned outreaches. We realised this was an attack from the enemy. He wanted to stop the Gospel outreach at all costs because so many people were being saved and healed. We finished the task God had called us to do and came home rejoicing, thankful that the Lord had protected our loved ones from harm.

Nehemiah had a similar experience. The devil used people to try and stop him from rebuilding the walls of Jerusalem. They prevailed on him to meet with them. Had he done so, he would have ended in a *cul-de-sac* because they planned to harm him. He was not ignorant of satan's devices. He said, *"I am doing a great work, so that I cannot come down. Why should the work cease while I leave it and go down to you?"* (Nehemiah 6:3)

Never give up on the tasks the Lord has called you to complete. Keep on keeping on, no matter the cost.

Finish what you start.

19

David Livingstone, Missionary and Explorer

*Also, I heard the voice of the Lord, saying: "Whom shall I send. And who will go for Us?"
Then I said, "Here am I! Send me."*
Isaiah 6:8

David Livingstone was a Scottish physician, explorer, and pioneer Christian missionary with the London Missionary Society. He heard the Call of God to Africa and never looked back. He left London in November 1840 on a ship bound for the Cape of Good Hope. David then trekked to Kuruman in South Africa to join Robert Moffatt at his Mission Station. Five years later, he married Mary, daughter of Robert Moffat whom he laid to rest in what is now known as Mozambique, dying of malaria.

Kuruman was not a very big town, and David Livingstone was frustrated. He felt there were enough churches there. He wanted to take the gospel to unreached areas, especially the vast plains to the north, motivated by reports of the smoke of a thousand villages where no missionary had ever been.

He left Kuruman and headed north. His travels took him through Botswana, Zimbabwe, and Zambia. David Livingstone had a passion for discovering the source of the Nile River. He believed his success would give him the influence to end the East African Arab–Swahili slave trade. He was ecstatic when he found it.

David Livingstone was the first European to cross the continent from west to east and to discover the Zambesi River, the Victoria Falls, and several major central African lakes. He wasn't the first white man to find the Victoria Falls, but he was the first to make it known. It is believed Portuguese explorers saw it first and, of course, the local African population knew about it. Its name in the local language means "the smoke that thunders." When you are about three kilometers away, you can feel the thunder of the falls under your feet. It's one of the most awesome sites I have ever seen.

David Livingstone preached the gospel wherever he went. He ministered in villages, under trees, in African huts, and wherever he could find people. He often sat on a blanket among the people dressed in his normal clothes. He never tried to change their culture. His mission was to change their way of life as they came to faith in the Lord Jesus Christ. The people loved him.

Some history books claim he only led one person to the Lord, but it is an interesting fact that the memory of David Livingston is still revered in Africa two hundred years later. Even dictators like Robert Mugabe did not dare remove statues erected in his honour, nor rename streets and towns that bear his name. The David Livingstone Secondary and Primary Schools has retained their names to this day.

This was a man who was committed to sharing the Gospel. David Livingstone buried his wife and two daughters on the mission field. He had many bouts of malaria, but stayed faithful to the end and died on his knees, praying.

His heart was removed and buried under a tree in his beloved Africa before his body was embalmed and sent home,

Are we as committed to the task the Lord has called us to accomplish for Him?

20
Divine Appointments

*The steps of a good man are ordered by the LORD, and
He delights in his way.*
Psalm 37:23

I was ministering in Western Cape, South Africa, many years ago. A well-known South African gospel singer was booked for the meetings. We had a meeting planned in the George Town Hall one evening and a large crowd was present. Sadly, as the meeting started, our singer had a very bad asthma attack and was hospitalised.

I was approached by one of the leaders. "There's a young man in the meeting who is willing to sing for you," he said. "Are you happy about that?"

It turned out to be a God Appointment. His name is Carl Erasmus. He sang two songs, and I was aware of a strong anointing on him. It was obvious he loved the Lord Jesus Christ and was singing from his heart. I sensed this young man would walk with me in the future.

Carl felt the same way. As I was preaching, he turned to his wife and said, "This is the man I want to minister with." After the meeting, he introduced himself. "I live in Benoni," he said. "When you get back to Johannesburg, I would like to come and talk to you."

When he visited my home, he brought his mother with him. She was ill and we laid hands on her in the Name of the Lord Jesus as we prayed. Christa was healed and we gave thanks. From that divine appointment, Carl and I have ministered together in many places. We have had over 27 healing meetings. Carl sings, I preach, and we both lay hands on the sick. We have seen many people healed over the years. This was definitely a case of the Lord ordering our steps.

Carl now lives in Australia. We have ministered together there too. We are still in close touch, and he regularly sings online via Zoom at our Sunday church meetings in London. It is such a joy to have a committed young man at my side and I thank the Lord, for setting him across my path.

I thank Him for everyone who is part of our *Messiah Ministries* team. You too are divine appointments. "Every time I think of you, I give thanks to my God. Whenever I pray, I make my requests for all of you with joy, for you have been my partners in spreading the Good News about Christ from the time you first heard of it until now" (Philippians 1:3-5).

Teamwork is very important in the ministry. Don't be a 'Lone Ranger'. Ask the Lord to send committed team members to support you in the work He has called you to do.

He has divine appointments for you too.

21

Doubt Weakens Faith

But let him ask in faith, with no doubting, for he who doubts is like a wave of the sea driven and tossed by the wind. For let not that man suppose that he will receive anything from the Lord.
James 1:6,7

Many people contact me from all over the world to pray for them. God is omniscient, omnipotent, and omnipresent. We may pray over the telephone or internet, via audio and text messages because the Lord Jesus Christ is not restricted by time, countries, or zones. The important thing is that we pray in faith. The Bible says, *"faith without works is dead"* (James 2:26). Faith is an active word. It is the "works" required to get answers to our prayers.

I was ministering in a large church in Pretoria. It was advertised as a *Healing Meeting* and a big crowd was present. I watched as people arrived, some in wheelchairs and on crutches. I thought, "Lord, these people want to see You in action. I'm glad You are the Healer, and not me."

After preaching the Word, I stepped down from the podium and started to move among the people as the Holy Spirit led. At one point, I walked towards a middle-aged woman in a wheelchair. Later I heard she had been in that wheelchair for over five years, unable to walk at all. Her husband stood behind her. As I came closer, she suddenly leapt out of the wheelchair and shouted, "Fergus, go and pray for other people. The Lord has just healed me!" I was about fifteen metres away and had not touched her or even prayed. She ran around the front of the church as people cheered her on. She came by faith and the Holy Spirit moved on her supernaturally. As we continued praying, many were healed.

I started working my way towards the other side of the church. I saw a beautiful young blond girl in her early twenties sitting in a wheelchair. Her parents and brother were standing behind her. As I walked towards her, the Holy Spirit spoke clearly to me. He said, "She is not going to stand up."

In this type of ministry, you must rely completely on the Holy Spirit. God is not like a machine you put coins into, and gum pops out. He is sovereign and we are just His servants.

I stopped to talk to her. She had been in an accident and was paralysed from the hips down. I told her I would pray for her, but that she would not be healed that night. She began to weep, and her parents looked at me in consternation. *"Why?"* demanded the father.

"You heard about this meeting," I responded quietly, "and you agreed to come just in case! You didn't believe God would heal her."

He looked at me as if I had hit him with a ten-pound hammer and began to weep. He knew it was the truth. There is a big difference between faith and presumption.

The Bible says, *"But without faith it is impossible to please*

Him, for he who comes to God must believe that He is, and that He is a rewarder of those who diligently seek Him" (Hebrews 11:6).

My earnest prayer for this young woman is that there may be a time when she will be healed and able to live a normal life.

22

Exercising Your Faith

Now faith is the substance of things hoped for, the evidence of things not seen.
Hebrews 11:1

We were in Bulawayo, Zimbabwe, for some meetings. Joanne and Eric van Dyk were with me. It was exciting for me to be there because I was born in Zimbabwe, then called Southern Rhodesia.

One evening we were ministering at an Old Age Home. There were about 80 residents and visitors present. They came to hear the Word of God and many also came to seek prayer for healing. I noticed one lady being wheeled in. She was very big and heavy and obviously could not walk. Her husband stood behind her.

"Pastor Buchan," she said, "I have been in this wheelchair for years. I want to walk again. Please pray for me."

I anointed her with oil, laid hands on her, and prayed the prayer of faith. I sensed the Holy Spirit ministering as I held out my hands to her. "Stand up, and come with me," I said.

She stood up and began walking. The hall was like one of the old school halls, with a metre high stage behind us. It was about 30 metres long. She walked halfway down the hall, turned around, and walked back. Her husband was in tears, the people present were crying, worshipping, and clapping. Everybody was very excited.

The next day her two daughters came to visit her at home. They were sceptical because their mother had been prayed for many times. They had given up on God and stopped going to church.

The girls called her on her mobile. "Hey, Mom, we are at the main gate. Please can you get someone to bring the keys?"

"OK," she said. "I will bring them."

She walked out of the front door and 25 metres down the garden. Their faces were a picture when she opened the gate and let them in. Those young ladies came back to church and rededicated their lives to the Lord Jesus Christ.

I've always said one miracle equals 1000 sermons. Healing miracles are especially powerful because people see their loved ones healed before their eyes and there can be no arguments.

The nine *Gifts of the Spirit* are still available to the Children of God. The era of miracles has not passed. In fact, the supernatural Gifts of the Spirit are more needed today than ever in this age of scepticism and doubt. The Lord said we are to *"pursue love and desire spiritual gifts"* (1 Corinthians 14:1).

Are you actively seeking the Lord for the Gifts of the Spirit to operate in your life?

23

Expect Persecution In These End Times

Then they will deliver you up to tribulation and kill you, and you will be hated by all nations for My name's sake.
Matthew 24:9

We go into the streets of London every Saturday morning to share the Gospel and pray for the sick, the homeless, the lost, alcoholics, drug addicts, and prostitutes. Joanne and I set off on Saturday, October 7, 2023, as usual, eager to lead many to Christ.

We approached a homeless man sitting on the pavement eating a big hamburger someone had given him. He was a white Englishman and he looked at us with interest as I greeted him.

"Good morning, Sir," I said. "How are you doing?"

"I'm battling," he responded. "But at least I have something to eat."

"Well, that's good," I replied. "I would like to pray for you."

"Oh, yes," he said. "I would like that."

My mission is to lead people to Christ. I started talking to him about repentance and receiving the Lord Jesus Christ as his Personal Saviour.

The moment I mentioned the Name of Jesus Christ, the man became aggressive and abusive. He started screaming and shouting at me so loudly that people passing by stopped and stared at us. They probably thought I had abused him in some way. This is the second time in three weeks I have experienced this. It reminds me of the Lord's words that believers will be hated by the world for His Name's sake.

I want to make a special point here. People seldom react when you talk about God. They love it when you say something like, "God bless you!" or "God loves you!" There are many so-called 'gods' in this world, but *"there is only one Mediator between God and men, the Man Christ Jesus"* (1 Timothy 2:3).

I always make a point of mentioning Jesus Christ, Son of God, when I minister to people. There are no grey areas when I speak to them. They know exactly who I'm talking about. That upsets a lot of people, and they often react badly. The devil and his evil spirits hate His Name. Expect persecution when you speak His Name, especially in these end times.

I want to challenge you today never to be ashamed of mentioning the Name of the Lord Jesus Christ, Son of God, when you speak to people. Always make it clear Who you stand for. The Lord Jesus Christ died for us and saved us. Now we are His Ambassadors with a commission to share the Gospel. *"Now then, we are ambassadors for Christ, as though God were pleading through us: we implore you on Christ's behalf, be reconciled to God"* (2 Corinthians 5:20).

Be encouraged by this promise of Jesus. *"Blessed are*

you when they revile and persecute you, and say all kinds of evil against you falsely for My sake. Rejoice and be exceedingly glad, for great is your reward in heaven, for so they persecuted the prophets who were before you" (Matthew 5:11,12).

24

Expect to be Offended

Then He said to the disciples, "It is impossible that no offenses should come, but woe to him through whom they do come!"
Luke 17:1

Joanne and I were out on the streets of London ministering to the homeless, the sick, alcoholics, drug addicts, and prostitutes. We were on Oxford Street and had a glorious time of ministry as seven people from different nationalities gave their lives to the Lord Jesus Christ. Our hearts were full of joy.

As we moved on, I saw a young English man. He didn't look in very good shape and I stopped to talk to him. "Hello," I said, "How are you doing?"

"I'm not too good," he said.

"I can see that. I think we need to pray."

His expression changed. "Pray to who?" he responded aggressively.

"Pray to the Lord Jesus Christ," I said.

The moment he heard the Name of Jesus, that young man

began to blaspheme His Name and swear at me. Jesus said expect offenses, but woe to those through whom they come. Many years ago, I would have taken offence at his attitude, but my heart went out to him because he was so lost. He was in a place no one should be. Sadly, there was nothing more I could do for him.

"Okay, son," I said. "I will leave you as you are. I pray that someday, someone will come to you and your heart will be softened enough to receive the Lord Jesus Christ." And I moved on.

Never be intimidated by rejection. Always be ready to stand out as a believer. If you are in the company of unbelievers and you want to thank the Lord for your meal, say your grace unashamedly. When everyone around you is drinking alcohol, order your Coca-Cola without shame. Make your stand for the Lord Jesus Christ without being "religious" or arrogant. Expect to be offended, but do not take offense. Leave the offense with Jesus and move on.

We have been left here on this earth to be witnesses to the One who died for us and whose Name opens the door to heaven. *"Nor is there salvation in any other, for there is no other name under heaven given among men by which we must be saved"* (Acts 4:12).

Do not be afraid to offend people with the Name of the Lord Jesus Christ. He is their only Hope. Those who respond to the Lord because of your witness will be glad for all eternity. Be encouraged as you step out for the Lord Jesus Christ.

Be strong and brave in the Power of His might.

25
Faith in Action

So then faith comes by hearing, and hearing by the word of God.
Romans 10:17

Joanne and I were invited to minister in an outlying village in a very rural area in northern Kenya. I stood on a large mound of packed sand to preach. There was a big gully in front of me with villages on both the right and left, as well as little shops. As I started preaching, the people got excited. They tore branches off the banana trees and started dancing in circles.

When I made the altar call, hundreds came forward to give their lives to Jesus. I noticed a man hobbling towards me on his stumps. His name was Richard. He had no legs, and his upper body was very large. He had a reputation for being a very fierce and angry man.

"Pastor, pray for me," he shouted in *Swahili* as he clamped his arms tightly around my right leg. He believed God would meet with him and he put his faith into action. He must have come at least one hundred metres on those stumps before he got to the top of the mound.

As I moved around praying for people, Richard clung to my leg and kept shouting. Finally, he calmed down. I put my hands on his head and prayed for him. The Holy Spirit moved powerfully upon him and Richard received the Lord Jesus as his Personal Saviour, still clinging to my leg.

"Tomorrow, I am preaching at that little church you can see from here. Will you come?"

"Yes," he said. "I will come. I want you to pray for work for me." He was a cobbler by trade but had no work.

The next morning, we arrived for the service and when I entered the church, there was Richard sitting in the front row. He was wearing his best pair of shorts, and his face was shining. We asked the Lord to give him some work and he went on his way rejoicing.

Monday morning, we were packing our cars to go home when I heard a voice outside the hut where Joanne and I were staying. It was Richard. This time he was shouting with joy. The Lord had honoured his prayer for work, and he was ecstatic.

What a difference the Gospel of the Lord Jesus Christ makes.

26
Given to Hospitality

Rejoicing in hope, patient in tribulation, continuing steadfastly in prayer; distributing to the needs of the saints, given to hospitality.
Romans 12:12,13

A few years ago, Fraser and I were ministering in a rural area in the northwestern part of Kenya. One of the women invited out team to spend the night in her home and we accepted gladly. It was a small house, but not yet completely built. She boiled some water in a bucket on an open fire. Then she placed the bucket and a candle on a small table under a tree and handed me a towel. "No one is going to see you, Sir" she said. "You can bath here."

Our host put two mattresses on the floor for Fraser and the three Pastors accompanying us. "Follow me," she said as she headed down a passageway to a small room. Her teenage daughter was sleeping there. "The Pastor needs your bed," she said. The young girl rose immediately without one word of complaint to allow some white guy to take over her bed. It reminded me of 1 Peter 4:9, which says, *"Be hospitable to one another without grumbling"* (1 Peter 4:9). I wonder how many of our Western teenagers would be so obliging. I was quite happy to sleep on the floor with the others, but she would have none of it. It was freezing cold, and the warm bed was a real blessing.

The next morning, she woke us for breakfast. "You must have something to eat before you leave." She said, "Breakfast is ready." We enjoyed a feast of mangoes, roasted peanuts, and cups of black tea. The hospitality of African people is amazing and something we should take note of. They are so willing to share the little they have. We were very grateful for her hospitality.

Hebrews 13:2 exhorts us to "not forget to entertain strangers, for by so doing some have unwittingly entertained angels." We certainly were not angels, but I know that lady and her family will receive their reward from the Lord Himself for their obedience to the leading of the Holy Spirit.

The Lord Jesus said, *"For whoever gives you a cup of water to drink in My Name, because you belong to Christ, assuredly, I say to you, he will by no means lose his reward"* (Mark 9:41).

"Therefore, as we have opportunity, let us do good to all, especially to those who are of the household of faith" (Galatians 6:10).

27

Giving Thanks

When you have eaten and are full, then you shall bless the LORD your God for the good land which He has given you.
Deuteronomy 8:10

I know this scripture talks about giving thanks once you have eaten, but I want to encourage you to give thanks even before you eat. We usually call that "saying Grace."

We were ministering in Kenya outside of Kitale, a very rural area. The team left early in the morning because we had quite a long journey ahead of us, so we had a bit of fruit before departing. When we arrived at our destination, we started work immediately and were busy most of the morning. By the time lunchtime arrived, we were starving.

"Would you like to have lunch with us?" the Headman's wife asked. We were more than happy, and the three pastors and I sat under a tree while we waited for our meal. We each received a very small bowl of steaming rice, a tablespoon of peas, and a small bottle of distilled water. They were a poor community, and we were very grateful, especially when we noticed our hosts did not have anything to eat. We gave thanks to the Lord first, and then thanked our hosts and prayed with them. We were so aware these people had nothing, and they had generously given us all they had available.

Those same pastors, even when they only drink a cup of black tea with no sugar, always give thanks to the Lord first. How often do we enjoy a sandwich and a lovely cup of coffee, but we don't give thanks? We don't even think about it. I was very challenged by their attitude of gratitude.

To this day, I cannot eat or drink anything without giving thanks. My mind always goes back to that village and the husband and wife who gave us their meal.

Jesus healed ten lepers one day and He was saddened that only one returned to give thanks. *"Were there not ten cleansed?" He asked. "But where are the nine? Were there not any found who returned to give glory to God except this foreigner?" And He said to him, "Arise, go your way. Your faith has made you well"* (Luke 17:17-19).

This man received not only commendation from the Lord, but it seems He received something extra. Perhaps the Lord also healed the effects the leprosy had left in his body. The Lord appreciates a thankful spirit. He hates grumbling and complaining.

Do you complain a lot, or are you grateful for even the smallest blessings the Lord has given you?

Show your gratitude by always taking the time to give thanks.

28

God Can Melt The Hardest Heart

The king's heart is in the hand of the LORD like the rivers of water; He turns it wherever He wishes.
Proverbs 21:1

I was a professional golfer for many years. Golfers are generally tough guys, focused on their game. If God can soften a king's heart, He can change any hard heart. He softened my heart and called me away from golf into full-time Christian ministry. I have seen Him change hearts radically over the years. There is one incident I will never forget. I was chatting with a tough professional sportsman about the things of God. He was unimpressed. This is how our conversation went.

"I don't believe all that stuff," he mocked.

"I believe your wife is a Christian."

"Yeah," he responded. "That's right."

"Your children are grown up and I heard they are Christians too."

"Yes," he said. I could see he wasn't sure where this conversation was going, and he looked at me with a puzzled look on his face.

"Well, tell me something. Do you love your wife and your kids?" I asked him.
"Of course, I do."
"Good," I responded. "Because I want you to enjoy your time with them."
"I do."

I looked him straight in the eye. "I mean, I really want you to enjoy your time with them because when you die you will never see them again!"

He looked shocked. "What do you mean?"

"It's very simple," I told him. "There are only two places we go when you die. One is for the believer – heaven. And the other one is for the unbeliever. He's going to hell, whatever hell is. But you're not going to be with your family again."

That is the reality at the end of the day. The Bible says: *"Enter by the narrow gate; for wide is the gate and broad is the way that leads to destruction, and there are many who go in by it. Because narrow is the gate and difficult is the way which leads to life, and there are few who find it"* (Matthew 7:13,14).

That man got such a fright, I could see the shock in his eyes as he came under Holy Spirit conviction. I'm glad to tell you that he repented and gave his life to Jesus.

We serve a gracious mighty God, but He is not to be played with or treated lightly. *"Therefore, as the Holy Spirit says, 'Today, if you will hear His voice, do not harden your hearts…'"* (Hebrews 3:7,8).

This life is our only opportunity to make peace with God.

29
God Has Your Back

Fear not, for I am with you; Be not dismayed, for I am your God. I will strengthen you. Yes, I will help you I will uphold you with My righteous right hand.
Isaiah 41:10

When you are in tough circumstances, do not panic. God has your back, and He knows how to work out every detail to your advantage when you trust Him.

I was returning to the UK after my latest mission in Southern Sudan in July 2023. David, my administrator, left for his home by bus, and Boutros drove me to the airport. His brother accompanied us. The Lord arranged for him to come because He was working all things together for my good.

Boutros dropped us off at the airport because he needed to go back to town. His brother decided to see me off safely. The Juba airport is still not completed and is a bit chaotic. I had to go to one section for passport control, another to go through security, and still another to go into the waiting room. Boutros' brother waited patiently while I went to get my passport stamped.

The Passport Control officer took my passport and was

about to stamp it when he looked at me in consternation. "You have overstayed your welcome here," he said. "You are here one day more than your visa allows."

"That's not possible," I protested. "Look for yourself," he said. I was shocked to see the Embassy in London had made an error with the date. An administrator was called. "You have a problem," he said. "You cannot board this plane."

I was tired and hot after ten days of intense mission work in the bush and not feeling well. When I finally got to London, I discovered just what a serious condition I was in. God had my back and subsequently healed me completely. "I cannot miss this plane," I insisted.

"Well, you can buy another ticket," he said. I was past arguing. "Where can I find an ATM?"

"There are no ATMs in this airport," he said as he took my passport from me,

The Lord was working behind the scenes. C' brother was still waiting patiently. He called Boutros on his mobile and told him about my dilemma. Boutros promised to return to the airport immediately. I had given him a gift in dollars, and he offered to bring it to me.

The clock was ticking. I was praying and calling on the Lord Jesus for favour. Boutros was stuck in a traffic jam. Eventually, he parked the car and took a motorbike taxi to the airport. He arrived just as passport control was closing. We bought a visa, and my passport was stamped. Looking back as I ran to board the plane, I saw those two lovely Sudanese men waving goodbye. How I praised the Lord as we took off and headed back to London. He knows how to work everything together for good. Every detail was taken care of.

Trust Him to do that for you today.

30

God is No Respecter of Persons

"For My thoughts are not your thoughts, Nor are your ways My ways," says the LORD. "For as the heavens are higher than the earth, So are My ways higher than your ways, And My thoughts than your thoughts."
Isaiah 55:8-9

About fifty years ago, I was working as a young professional golfer at the *Nchanga Golf Club* on the copper belt in Zambia. I met a lot of good sportsmen and a group of us formed a close bond. We were young and full of fun, real rough diamonds in those days. We drank beer and socialized, as young people do, never dreaming that the Lord would call us into the ministry someday. None of us went to Church. We never talked about Jesus.

It is amazing how God uses divine connections. There was Harry Rose and his wife, Betty. Harry became a Commonwealth weightlifter. He wanted to learn to play golf and we connected. Angus, my brother, decided he wanted to become a weightlifter, so Harry took him under his wing and started training him. Angus was also an outstanding rugby player. Another divine connection was John and Jenny Rose.

Looking back to those early days, I am so blessed to see

where God has taken us. Harry and Betty Rose are strong Christians and are the godparents of our two daughters. John and Jenny planted a thriving church in Alberton, Johannesburg, South Africa. So, we have Angus Buchan, the Evangelist, Fergus Buchan, the Missionary, and John Rose, the Pastor, in fulltime Christian ministry out of that little group. We are still the best of friends.

It is amazing to think God anointed us to reach hundreds of thousands for Jesus. Never despise small beginnings. You never know what potential the Lord has put into the people you meet or what His plans and purposes are for their lives.

There is a beautiful song about King David of old. It says *'when others saw a shepherd boy, God saw a king'.* What potential does the Lord see when He looks at you? Are you willing to dedicate yourself fully to Him so that He may guide you into the person He birthed you to be?

We are fearfully and wonderfully made by the Lord for a purpose. May His handiwork not be wasted because we want to do things our way. God's thoughts and ways are nothing like ours. He is no respecter of persons.

Why not take a moment to re-dedicate yourself to the Lord right now?

31
God Wants You To Forgive, No Matter the Circumstances

For if you forgive men their trespasses, your heavenly Father will also forgive you. But if you do not forgive men their trespasses, neither will your Father forgive your trespasses.
Matthew 6:14-15

Zimbabwe was in dire straits and the people were starving. They had no food or diesel, and death was staring them in the face. Fraser and I packed our Landrover and trailer full of supplies, including food and diesel, before setting off on our mission trip to that struggling country.

There were issues at the Zimbabwe border post, and we finally got through very late at night. We pulled into a Holiday Inn just outside Messina. We usually slept rough in rural areas but decided to sleep in the little hotel that night. We had a long day ahead of us. We felt very uneasy about leaving our laden vehicle in the carpark, but it looked like a secure place. The grounds were fenced, and a security guard was on duty.

When we awoke the next morning, we were shocked to see our Landrover and trailer had been broken into during the night. All our food and supplies were gone. So was our spare diesel. They even drained our tank. We were angry. These supplies were meant for the very people who stole from us. It felt like a nightmare. We had just enough diesel to get to Bulawayo.

It was not easy to forgive those who stole from us. We were rightfully angry, but we decided to obey the Word of God. The Lord tells us clearly in Matthew 6:14,15 that we must forgive men their trespasses, and our heavenly Father will also forgive us our trespasses. If we refuse to be obedient, there are consequences. It was a wake-up call. We forgave them because that is what the Lord told us to do.

Fraser and I survived on pasta, watermelon, and boiled eggs for the next three days. The Lord showed us His mercy as believers who heard of our plight brought us food and diesel. That enabled us to complete our mission and bring God's Word to a people without hope.

A similar thing happened to one of Africa's greatest missionaries, David Livingstone. Some of his helpers stole his belongings one night. Among his stolen possessions was his medicine chest. It contained the valuable Quinine medication used to treat Malaria. David subsequently died of Malaria and his body was found in a kneeling position beside his bed. I am sure he forgave those who had caused him such distress.

By the grace of God, we were able to reach countless hundreds of souls as we travelled further north, preaching the Gospel and praying for the sick wherever we went. Looking back, we realize that we gave the people far more than what we had intended initially. We didn't have much food or diesel, but we gave them eternal hope through the preaching of the Word of God, which is far more precious.

Had we refused to forgive and returned home in anger, that could never have happened.

Is there someone you need to forgive?

32

God's Protection

For He shall give His angels charge over you, To keep you in all your ways.
Psalm 91:11

We were ministering in the south-eastern side of Uganda, very close to Lake Victoria. The area is a Muslim stronghold, and very remote. The nearest town was about two hours away. We slept on three-inch sponge mattresses spread on the floor of a half-finished house. There were no doors, windows, or even windowpanes and I was glad to have my own mosquito net.

We were busy with a three-day campaign when the owner of the house prevailed on me to visit her father. "We will organise a taxi to get you to his home," she said. I wasn't too happy, but she insisted. The taxi turned out to be a 50cc motorbike. The taxi driver was on the front seat, David in the middle, and I was on the back. We were travelling along the banks of a major tributary of Lake Victoria when we hit a pothole. The driver went over the top of the motorbike, David landed in a bush, and I was thrown down a very steep bank into the river. My hat went floating down the river, my mobile phone was waterlogged, and I was full of mud and dirt. Afterwards, they told me there were lots of crocodiles and snakes in that river.

As David pulled me out of the river, he said, "What's wrong with your wrist?" I looked down to see my right hand was dislocated from the wrist socket. Before I knew what was happening, he grabbed my wrist and pulled hard. I heard a loud crack as it slipped back into position. Well, that was the end of our proposed visit. We went back home to change and prepare for the evening meeting. I was in agony. I couldn't stand up to preach and looked like the *Hunchback of Notre Dame.* Sleeping on that foam mattress was an unforgettable experience. Many gave their lives to Christ, and it was worth the pain.

I know the Lord sent His angels to protect me from serious harm. The nearest hospital in Kampala was four hours away. If I had broken an arm or a leg, I would have been in serious trouble. I praise the Lord for sending His angels to look after me that day so we could continue to share the Gospel. The Bible tells us that the angels are *"ministering spirits sent forth to minister to those who will inherit salvation"* (Hebrews 1:14).

Always pray first before setting out on your day's activities. When I am home, we always pray together before the family leaves the house. Trust the Lord to protect and keep you and your loved ones from all evil.

33

Have You Felt Like Giving Up Lately?

Therefore, my beloved brethren, be steadfast, immovable, always abounding in the work of the Lord, knowing that your labor is not in vain in the Lord.
1 Corinthians 15:58

We were in Zimbabwe with quite a big team, including my son, Fraser, and Marta his wife. We drove from South Africa to Bulawayo, then to Livingstone, home of the famous Victoria Falls, and travelled inland towards Harare. We were heading for a large village in a rural area.

They were expecting us on a particular day in the late afternoon for a three-day ministry visit. We left early in the morning but got totally lost. There are no roads to speak of or signals available for mobile phones deep in the bush. The meeting was scheduled for five o'clock in the afternoon and there was no way to tell them we were running late or that we were even on the way. I can still picture us with machetes cutting down trees in the pitch dark so the truck could get through. We didn't know where we were at times but just kept going. Eventually, we arrived at the right village. We were nearly eight hours late. It was well after midnight.

About sixty people were seated on makeshift seats, singing and praising God as they waited. The chairs looked like catapults, just two poles in a V formation with a pole in the centre to sit on. No one had left and gone home. They just waited patiently. No one complained or questioned why we were so late. When they saw the lights of the truck, they sang and rejoiced even louder. They were expectant and excited.

We were exhausted but we opened the side of the truck and switched on the lights powered by our generator. I preached with every bit of energy I had left, and the Holy Spirit touched the hearts of those precious people. At the end of the service, everyone stood to acknowledge they were receiving the Lord Jesus Christ as their Personal Saviour. We had a joyous three days of anointed ministry in that village. I'm so glad they waited with anticipation to hear the Word of God, and we persevered in the strength and power of the Lord. Giving up and turning back was never an option.

Have you thought about giving up lately? Spend some time meditating on 1 Corinthians 15:58. We must keep on keeping on because our labour is never in vain in the Lord. When we do the possible, He does the impossible.

May I encourage you to wait on the Lord and not become discouraged or despondent? Be steadfast and immovable, abounding (going the extra mile) as you labour for Him.

Never give up!

34

How to Handle Bribes

You shall not pervert justice, nor take a bribe, for a bribe blinds the eyes of the wise and twists the words of the righteous.
Deuteronomy 16:19

We were ministering in Southern Sudan in July 2023. Sudan is a war-torn area, and we encountered many roadblocks as we travelled through the country. One day we were stopped at a roadblock manned by the army and police. A young soldier approached the car and asked Butrus our driver, for our documents. "Who is this white man?" he said.

"He's a pastor from London," Butrus replied. "He's come to do ministry."

The soldier stared at me and abruptly walked back to his guard hut on a hill. We didn't know what to think as we waited. Suddenly he motioned to Butrus to join him. We watched as an animated conversation ensued. "Unless we give him something," Butrus told us, "He says he will not let us through."

"No, I am not giving him a bribe," I said emphatically. "The Lord will take care of this."

Back he went up the hill to the guard hut. After more arguing, Butrus came back with a new message. "He saw the *Messiah Ministries* caps and t-shirts in the car and says he will let us through if we give him some."

"I am giving him nothing," I said. Another trip to the guard hut and after some very loud conversation, Butrus returned. "He says he wants some water if you want to go through."

It was very hot, and we were all getting frustrated, but I was determined not to bribe my way through the roadblock. Up the hill went Butrus again and tempers flared. We waited in the hot car.

Eventually, the soldier came out of his guard hut and reluctantly lifted the boom. Butrus was laughing. "He says to tell you that you are a very hard man, and he will never come to your church!"

Trust the Lord always in all circumstances. He knows how to handle every type of situation. Don't let a bribe take your eyes off Jesus.

John 16:33 says *"These things I have spoken to you, that in Me you may have peace. In the world you will have tribulation; but be of good cheer, I have overcome the world."*

We can trust our sovereign, almighty, powerful God to make a way, even when there seems to be no way.

35

I Was Blind But Now I See

I, the LORD, have called You in righteousness, And will hold Your hand; I will keep You and give You as a covenant to the people, As a light to the Gentiles, To open blind eyes, To bring out prisoners from the prison, Those who sit in darkness from the prison house.
Isaiah 42:6-7

Many years ago, before I was saved, I was a young golf professional at the *Nchanga* Golf Club on the Copper Belt, very close to the Congo border. I was about 19-years-old. A fellow golf professional and I used to play squash every afternoon to keep fit. We were both good players and being golfers, we could really hit that squash ball.

I hit the ball and was watching him as he ran to return it. Before I knew what was happening, the squash ball hit me directly in the eye. I was in absolute agony as I fell to the ground. They rushed me to the local hospital and put me in a general ward. My eye was bleeding very badly, and I was devastated when I heard the doctors saying they may have to remove my eye. That would have meant the end of my professional golfing career. They bound both my eyes with a bandage, and I lay there in the darkness, blinded both physically and spiritually.

I was the only White man in the hospital ward. I could hear

children screaming and the sound of chickens running around the ward. I felt so lonely and miserable. I sensed someone at my bedside and heard a beautiful voice saying in English, "Are you in pain?"

"I am," I groaned.

"I'm American," she said. "Where are you from?"

That lovely nurse took excellent care of me. She found a single bed in a private room and moved me out of the general ward. In those days I was an arrogant racist and didn't have much time for Black people. I had no idea who she was or what racial group she belonged to. I just loved her voice. She was so kind and gentle.

As they were taking me to the operating theatre to remove my eye, a specialist from Libya happened to be visiting. He stopped to look at me. "What's wrong with this man?" he asked. He took the bandages off my eyes and examined my wound.

"No," he told the doctors. "Don't remove his eye. I will inject his eyeball. He has an excellent chance of recovery."

When he finished, they bandaged my eyes again and sent me back to the ward. A day or so later, the doctors were back. "The specialist has gone back to Libya," they said. "He told us to remove your bandages."

The Lord had a plan and purpose for my life before I even knew Him. My eyes took a long time to heal, but I have two very good eyes as a testimony to the Lord's gracious help.

I looked around. The doctors were Black. The nurses were Black.

"Who is my nurse?" I asked them.

An African American nurse smiled at me. I don't remember her name, but I will always remember her face. My dearest hope is that I will meet that young nurse in heaven one day. She literally saved my life.

From that day onwards, my heart towards Black people changed. I love them like I love my own people and I have spent many years sharing the Gospel across Africa. I have a passion for these beautiful people.

When I met the Lord Jesus Christ as my own personal Saviour and Lord, He opened my spiritual eyes. I can truthfully say, once I was blind (physically and spiritually), but now I see. I no longer see the colour of people's skin. I see only saved people and lost people. I hope you do too.
 some notes. This is what he wrote:

In Times of Trouble, say:

36

In Time of Trouble, Say...

*Call upon Me in the day of trouble; I will deliver you,
and you shall glorify Me.*
Psalm 50:15

A great man of God from South Africa, Andrew Murray, was invited to minister in London at four big meetings some 180 years ago. When he finished his last meeting, his hosts took him to Wimbledon, where he was staying.

When they walked in the door, he saw a letter on the table addressed to Reverend Andrew Murray. It was from a well-known Pastor who had been at the meetings. When he opened the letter, Andrew Murray was taken aback as he was berated and ridiculed. "The best place for you is to go back to South Africa," wrote the man angrily. His hosts were highly upset and wanted to immediately take this man to task.

Andrew Murray picked up the letter. "I won't have dinner," he said. "I must go to my room." There he called on the Lord in his day of trouble. The Presence of the Holy Spirit was very tangible as he read Psalm 50:15 and made some notes. This is what he wrote:

In Times of Trouble, say:

- First, He brought me here. It is by His will I am in this strait place. In that fact, I will rest.
- Next, He will keep me here in His love and give me grace to behave as His child.
- Then, He will make the trial a blessing, teaching me the lessons he intends me to learn and working in me the grace He means to bestow.
- Last, In His good time, He can bring me out again. How and when He knows.

Let me say, I am here:

1. By His appointment
2. In His keeping
3. Under His training
4. For His time

The next day he took the letter and visited the Pastor. They talked a while and then prayed together. As a result of that meeting, the man became one of Andrew Murray's life-long friends.

Like Andrew Murray, I don't like talking on the 'phone when I have confrontational issues. I like to talk to people one-on-one and see their eyes. This is a scriptural principle. If you have an issue with a fellow believer, approach them first. If there is no reconciliation, take two or three witnesses. If the issue persists and you wish to take it further, approach the leadership of the church (Matthew 18:15-17). *"If it is possible, as much as depends on you, live peaceably with all men"* (Romans 12:18).

Always remember, you are called to please God and not man when you are unfairly attacked or criticised. Call on the Lord in the day of trouble and He will help you.

37

Jesus Is Still The Healer

Then Jesus went about all the cities and villages, teaching in their synagogues, preaching the gospel of the Kingdom, and healing every sickness and every disease among the people.
Matthew 9:35

A few years ago, I was ministering in Zimbabwe. We were holding three days of healing meetings in a little town called Kadoma. On the third day, several people with hearing problems were present. Among them was an Irish lady. She was a Matron and had come specifically for prayer. She was totally deaf in both ears.

The Lord showed me how to lay hands on the deaf and minister to them and many ears were opened that day. The meeting went on for several hours. There were so many people wanting prayer, I could not get to everyone individually and I missed the Matron.

I was exhausted when we closed the service and retreated to the Pastor's vestry. Suddenly there was a loud knock at the door and there stood that big Irish lady, "You forgot to pray for me," she said. "I am not leaving until you do."

I laid my hands on her ears and started praying. "What can

you hear?" I asked. "Don't shout at me!" she responded. "I can hear perfectly." Both her ears were opened. That lady had faith. She gave me the biggest hug I have ever had from a granny. What a wonderful time we had rejoicing.

Jesus once asked two blind men who came for prayer, *"Do you believe that I am able to do this?" "Yes, Lord,"* they responded. *"Then He touched their eyes, saying, 'According to your faith let it be to you.' And their eyes were opened"* (Matthew 9:28-30). As an old song says, Prayer is the Key to Heaven, but it's Faith that unlocks the door."

The Lord loves to confirm His Word with signs following. He had compassion on people when He walked this earth, and He still has compassion today. *"But when He saw the multitudes, He was moved with compassion for them, because they were weary and scattered, like sheep having no shepherd"* (Matthew 9:36).

Why are we not seeing more miracles today? Jesus said, *"The harvest truly is plentiful, but the laborers are few. Therefore pray the Lord of the harvest to send out laborers into His harvest"* (Matthew 9:17).

Are you willing to be an answer to that prayer? Are you ready to share His Word, and allow Him to confirm that Word with signs following? It is not an easy ministry, but there is nothing more exciting than to see the Lord confirming His Word as He meets the needs of weary people in body, soul, and spirit.
Will you be a labourer for Jesus?

38

Living In Unity

Behold, how good and how pleasant it is for brethren to dwell together in unity! It is like the precious oil upon the head, running down on the beard, the beard of Aaron, running down on the edge of his garments. It is like the dew of Harmon, dew descending upon the mountains of Zion; For there the LORD commanded the blessing – Life forevermore.
Psalm 133:1-3

This is a very short Psalm. It has only three verses, but it carries a powerful truth. God commands His blessing where there is unity. It is vital that we live in unity, especially in our families, the workplace, and in the church. We must stand together in these perilous times we are living in. We need each other, whether in a big or small ministry. *"All of you together are Christ's body, and each of you is a part of it"* (1 Corinthians 12:27).

When believers stand together in unity, blessing always follows. Disunity results in fighting one another and arguing over vision, goals, and methods. How can God bless a group when they are divided? We spent time fasting and praying until the Lord revealed to us His Will for *Messiah Ministries*. We are united in our efforts to reach the lost on the streets of London, and in areas our teams minister, as well as the unreached areas of Africa. And the Lord is adding His blessing to the work.

It is the same in marriage. If you are not in unity with your spouse, there will be disunity in the family. If we want our prayers answered, we must be in unity concerning what we pray about. That is why the Bible says we must not be unequally yoked with unbelievers. That always leads to trouble because unity is the key to blessing. Talk to your Pastor or a mature Christian before choosing your life partner. Marriage is difficult enough without being unequally yoked.

Abraham had the right attitude. When there were issues with Lot, he said: *"Please let there be no strife between you and me, and between my herdsmen and your herdsmen; for we are brethren. Is not the whole land before you? Please separate from me. If you take the left, then I will go to the right; or, if you go to the right, then I will go to the left"* (Genesis 13:8,9). Abraham wanted the blessing of God on his life, more than he wanted his own way.

Gordon Lindsay of Christ for the Nations said: "It is always my policy to give in on non-essentials. It is only on essentials where I feel that the Will of God is at stake that I am adamant."

Is the Holy Spirit speaking to you about an issue in your life causing a lack of unity? Deal with it today.

39

Madame Guyon, a Life Transformed Through Prayer

Be anxious for nothing, but in everything by prayer and supplication, with thanksgiving, let your requests be made known to God; and the peace of God, which surpasses all understanding, will guard your hearts and minds through Christ Jesus.
Philippians 4:6,7

Madame Jeanne Guyon was a French Christian accused of advocating Quietism, a form of Christian mysticism focusing the mind and soul on silent spiritual contemplation and prayer. The Quietist movement was considered heretical by the Roman Catholic Church and Madame Guyon was imprisoned from 1695 to 1703 after publishing the book *A Short and Very Easy Method of Prayer.*

Imprisoned and living in solitary confinement inside the infamous Bastille prison for seven years, Madame Guyon wrote that she passed her time there in great peace and was content to spend the rest of her life imprisoned if that was God's will. She sang songs of praise to God during her imprisonment. She explained that because her heart was so full of joy that God gave her, she even viewed the stones of the prison as if they were beautiful rubies. Her autobiography and devotional writings have mentored thousands of people over the years, teaching them to pray and develop a rich relationship with Christ, even in the worst of circumstances.

Forced to marry Jacques Guyon when she was just sixteen, she endured twelve years of misery from both her husband and his domineering mother. They had no children and when she became a widow, Madame Guyon devoted her life to pursuing a deep inner life with Christ through prayer, serving the poor, and travelling throughout Europe to serve and teach. She wrote books about prayer. This was a woman of great faith.

Madame Guyon made a statement that I've never forgotten. She wrote, "Great faith produces great abandonment." By that, she meant that great faith enables us to accept all that happens to us as coming, not from the hand of man, but from God Himself.

Job believed that too. He said, *"Shall we indeed accept good from God, and shall we not accept adversity?"* (Job 2:10).

So did Joseph. *"But as for you, you meant evil against me; but God meant it for good, in order to bring it about as it is this day, to save many people alive"* (Genesis 50:20). That kind of faith only comes from spending quality time with the Lord Jesus Christ in prayer and meditating on His Word.

How is your Quiet Time?

40

Making Wise Decisions

Where there is no counsel, the people fall; But in the multitude of counselors there is safety.
Proverbs 11:14

The Bible gives us very wise counsel about making decisions. We are not aware of all the facts surrounding situations and we often lack experience. That is why we should always consult others we trust. Obviously, we hear from the Lord first, but we also need the counsel of others in the outworking of our plans.

When we pray about our outreaches as Messiah Ministries, I always take time to consult with my team. I might have received five invitations, but I can't be in five places at once. As a team, we pray together as we seek the Lord's will. My wife, our leaders, and I consult with each other because we realise the importance of unity. We must stand together and support one another in every outreach. We are not looking for opinions and advice, but a clear sense of the leading of the Holy Spirit. Where there is no counsel, failure is certain. In consultation with others of like spirit, there is safety.

Messiah Ministries has an inner core I work with very closely. Obviously, with our type of ministry, we have believers in our fellowship who come and go for various reasons. Some move to other towns and countries, but there is that inner core I pray with and trust their counsel. It is not wise to be a lone wolf. Ministry is a team effort, and we need all our various gifts and abilities to work together. Our bodies function the same way. Every member has a part to play and, together, we can achieve much.

There are also dedicated intercessors from many countries who pray with us every week. I have the privilege of being able to ask them to pray for a specific outreach or need. I don't make decisions on my own. Once I have heard from the Lord, we seek confirmation together.

That principle is true for every home, family, and decisions that affect your life. Perhaps you must undergo a major operation, but you don't feel peace about it. Approach your spiritual leaders and ask them to pray with you. Let's pray together and believe together. I urge you to stay in fellowship, stay in unity, and support one another. Where there is unity, the Lord commands His blessing (Psalm 133:1-3).

The twelve disciples were a team with the Lord Jesus. One fell and had to be replaced, but the rest were unified in Christ. After His ascension they continued to have a powerful and effective ministry because they remained united. These Spirit-filled men changed the world. If they had surrounded themselves with their own little groups, split from one another, and gone their own way, things would have been very different. God added His blessing because they were united. They met together, prayed about everything, and shared their lives.

Listen to the Word of God, adhere to it, and put it into action. Blessing will be the result.

41

Mean What You Say

But let your 'Yes' be 'Yes,' and your 'No,' No.' For whatever is more than these is from the evil one.
Matthew 5:37

Many years ago, an elderly Pastor gave me a word of wisdom. He said, "Fergus, if you say you're going to pray for somebody, you had better pray for them. Because if you say you will, and you don't, that makes you a liar."

The Lord Jesus said that satan is the source of all lies. *"He was a murderer from the beginning, and does not stand in the truth, because there is no truth in him. When he speaks a lie, he speaks from his own resources, for he is a liar and the father of it"* (John 8:44).

The world we live in today is full of confusion. It is filled with people-pleasers, who say one thing and do another. Some say things they shouldn't say. Faith gives way to distrust. *"If someone says, 'I love God,' and hates his brother, he is a liar; for he who does not love his brother whom he has seen, how can he love God whom he has not seen?"* (John 4:20).

The Bible is clear. *"But the cowardly, unbelieving, abominable, murderers, sexually immoral, sorcerers, idolaters, and all liars shall have their part in the lake which burns with fire and brimstone, which is the second death"* (Revelation 21:8).

If you say, "Yes, I can do that for you," the Lord expects you to do it. Problems come when people say, "Yes, we will take care of it" and a week later it still has not happened. Confusion, anger, disputes, and disrespect are the outcome. Rather be honest and say, "No, I can't do it." Let your Yes be Yes, and your No, No. Repent of all lies you have told and receive the Lord's forgiveness. Make a commitment today to do everything in your power to follow through. The Lord commends those who *"keep their promises even when it hurts"* (Psalm 15:4 NLT).

"Do not let your mouth cause your flesh to sin, nor say before the messenger of God that it was an error. Why should God be angry at your excuse and destroy the work of your hands?" (Ecclesiastes 5:6).

Ananias and Sapphira, an early Church couple, discovered too late that God does not appreciate liars. They promised the leaders that they would pay the proceeds of a house they were selling to the church funds. When the sale was done, they kept back part of the proceeds and Peter challenged them. He said, *"Ananias, why has satan filled your heart to lie to the Holy Spirit… you have not lied to men but to God."* Their lies cost them their lives (Acts 5:1-11).

Here is a good prayer to pray: *"Let the words of my mouth and the meditation of my heart be acceptable in Your sight, O Lord, my strength and my Redeemer"* (Psalm 19:14).

42

More About Prayer

*Call to Me, and I will answer you, and show you great
and mighty things, which you do not know.*
Jeremiah 33:3

When we pray, the Lord will bring about His Will for our lives. God waits for our prayers. That is how He has chosen to work in our world. He loves it when we bring our petitions to Him in prayer because He wants to show us great and mighty things we could never know without spending time with Him.

Does He listen when an individual calls on Him? He certainly does. You don't have to be in a congregation, cell group, or ministry to have an audience with the Lord. You just simply call to Him, like I've done many, many times when I've had an urgent need on the mission field, for example. I really encourage you to get into a habit of praying about everything. Of course, there is tremendous power in praying together with others. The Lord promises to be present when two or three (or more) of His people are in agreement (Matthew 18:20).

How long should we pray? Martin Luther told his wife he had to get up an hour earlier the next morning to pray because he had an important meeting to attend and needed more time to consult with the Lord. Praying Hyde, a famous British intercessor, loved to spend long hours in prayer. You can visit his prayer room in London to see the indentations on the floor this godly man left with his knees. David and Daniel prayed three times a day. Nehemiah sent up quick prayers when he needed an immediate answer. There are no rules. The important thing is to pray consistently. Get up a little earlier for your *Quiet Time* or carve out some time in your day when you can keep your daily appointment with the Lord. I like to pray in the early hours. Many times, I also pray on the bus or tube as I travel to appointments.

What do we pray about? Whatever the Holy Spirit lays on our hearts. Pray for our church, the pastor, and fellow believers. Pray for our governments and our leaders, as we are called to do in Romans 13. Pray for those in need, our families, friends, relationships, work, all kinds of situations, and whatever is happening in our lives and our world. Pray about your own needs. He wants you to bring them to Him. He is your Heavenly Father.

Does the Lord always answer our prayers? He does, but you are not always going to get the answers you want. The Lord may say "yes," "no," or "wait" because He sees the bigger picture and we always bow to His sovereign will. James 4:2,3 tells us that *"you do not have because you do not ask."* At the same time, the Lord is not willing to answer prayers that are out of line with His Will for us. *"You ask and do not receive, because you ask amiss, that you may spend it on your pleasures"* (James 4:2-3). Prayer is hard work, but there is nothing more rewarding than seeing the Lord answer those prayers.

There are two very important conditions for answered prayer. First, we must pray in the Will of God. And, secondly, we must be living lives pleasing to the Lord, in word and deed. *"If I regard iniquity in my heart, the Lord will not hear"* (Psalm 66:18).

"Now to Him who is able to do exceedingly abundantly above all that we ask or think, according to the power that works in us, to Him be glory in the church by Christ Jesus to all generations, forever and ever. Amen" (Ephesians 3:20-21).

43

Moved by the Spirit

...knowing this first, that no prophecy of Scripture is of any private interpretation, for prophecy never came by the will of man, but holy men of God spoke as they were moved by the Holy Spirit.
2 Peter 1:20-21

True prophecy must always have its source in the Holy Spirit. While this scripture is referring specifically to the Written Word of God, it carries a divine principle. When men speak for God, it is vital that they are moved by the Holy Spirit and not by the desires of their own heart. False prophets imagine they speak for God and blame others when their words do not come to pass.

But what joy it brings when you know the Holy Spirit has indeed spoken and you watch the prophetic word you shared come to pass.

Joanne and I were on the border of northern Kenya on another mission trip. One Saturday I was ministering to a group of men and women. Many Elders and Pastors were also present. Suddenly, a man burst through the door. "I need a break," he wept. I could see he was not in a good place. His clothes were dirty, and he wore no shoes. His name was Tom.

Tom sat down and listened to the message, then he came forward for prayer. I sensed the presence of the Holy Spirit as He moved upon me. "I don't usually do this, Tom," I told him, "But I have a Word from the Lord for you. Tomorrow you are going to get a telephone call from a company that requires your expertise with pumps and irrigation."

"I receive that, Sir," he said, thanking me as he walked away.

The next morning, Tom appeared at the Sunday service. He looked a lot neater. "I have come to tell to tell you what has just happened," he said.

He was invited onto the platform. "This Pastor told me yesterday that I would receive a telephone call this morning. That is exactly what has happened. I have just got a call from a company who needs urgent help with some irrigation. I am signing the contract tomorrow morning."

Many years later, we were in the same area and Tom came to see me. He invited me to lunch. I was so blessed to see the man who had been destitute, now doing so well. He had a beautiful home, and a lovely wife and children. We enjoyed a sumptuous meal together and he gave me a financial gift for the ministry. God had completely restored him.

The cherry on top for me is that Tom is now an Elder in that very church.

If God can do that for Tom, He can do it for you.

"Delight yourself also in the LORD, And He shall give you the desires of your heart. Commit your way to the LORD, Trust also in Him, And He shall bring it to pass" (Psalm 37:4-5).

44

My Vision of Alistair

Blessed be the God and Father of our Lord Jesus Christ, the Father of mercies and God of all comfort who comforts us in all our tribulation that we may be able to comfort those who are in any trouble, with the comfort with which we ourselves are comforted by God.
2 Corinthians 1:4

Before I found Jesus, I was a so-called tough guy, ready to take on anyone and anything. After Alistair's accident, I couldn't stop crying, even though I had just given my heart to the Lord. The Lord has many ways of comforting His people. For me, it was with a supernatural vision.

One night about two weeks after the accident, I went to bed with a grieving heart and God gave me a vision. I know the difference between dreams and visions. I've had visions four times and heard the Lord speak to me audibly once. My vision of Alistair was very real. *It was not a dream.* I looked at my watch and it was exactly three o'clock in the morning.

In the vision, I saw Alistair running towards me. His broken body was completely healed and restored. He looked beautiful and the expression on his face was one of pure joy and happiness. Neither of us said anything. It was a short and silent vision, but I will never forget it. I've never seen that vision again, but I know Alistair is happy in heaven.

I woke the next morning in perfect peace and shared my experience with Joanne. Later my wife said she knew I had really seen Alistair because I stopped crying. The peace of God that passes understanding filled my being and Joanne saw the change in me. I understood what David meant when he said about his little son, *"Can I bring him back again? I shall go to him, but he shall not return to me"* (2 Samuel 12:23).

That supernatural vision began the restoration of our family as we came to terms with Alistair's homegoing. It brought us to a place where we can comfort and encourage others who have lost loved ones, especially children. It is important to keep our eyes on Jesus, no matter how we feel or what we are going through. The Lord will bring you through, with or without a vision. We all grieve differently but the Holy Spirit knows how to give believers the faith to know we will see our loved ones again one day.

No trial is ever wasted. He comforts us in all our troubles so that we can comfort others with the same comfort God has given us.

What are you experiencing that the Lord can use to help others?

45

Never Despise Small Beginnings

For who has despised the day of small things?
Zechariah 4:10

"Let's take some food to our brothers and sisters in Zimbabwe," my son Fraser said. Times were desperate in that country and people were literally starving. We prayed about it and eventually set off for Zimbabwe in a 5-ton pickup filled with as many supplies as we could carry. When we saw firsthand the enormity of the situation in northern Zimbabwe, our hearts were broken. How could these few supplies meet so much need?

The New Living Translation says, *"Do not despise these small beginnings, for the Lord rejoices to see the work begin…"* The challenge is to do something when the Lord shows you a situation. Begin, make a start, no matter how small.

When we got back to our small mission station in KwaZulu-Natal, we were determined to return with more supplies and shared the need with fellow believers. A good friend of mine, Erin Georgiou, published an article in *JOY Magazine* and the response was amazing. A believer in Durban who owned a trucking company contacted us. "I want to be on board," she said. "I will supply you with a

32-ton truck and a driver."

People started bringing supplies, including the local farmers. Churches got involved. They supplied maize (the staple diet of Africa), cooking oil, rice, sugar, tea, coffee, petrol, diesel, and much more. We added Bibles and tracts. The Lord touched so many hearts, it was exciting.

I visited a large pharmacy in Johannesburg to get some ointment for my eyes. While I was waiting, I was fascinated by a display of reasonably price generic spectacles with different strengths. They were new on the market. You don't need an eye test. Just find a pair that suits your eyes.

A salesman approached me, and we got chatting. "I am a missionary," I told him as I shared our vision. "We are taking supplies and Bibles to Zimbabwe. I love these glasses, especially for the elderly who can no longer read because of their poor eyesight." He gave me his card. "Call me later, I may be able to get some donated for your trip."

When I called him, he asked me to come in because the owner wanted to meet me. "I believe you are a missionary," he said. "My agent spoke to me about you."

We had a chat and then he picked up his intercom. "How many of those new spectacles can we release?"

"Can I give you a couple of hundred pairs?" he asked me. I was stunned, but he wasn't finished yet.

"What else do you need?"

I left there with painkillers, bandages, plasters, ointment, medical supplies, and 1000 pairs of spectacles!

If you're faithful with small things, God will trust you with bigger things. Never compare yourself to other people or other ministries. Just be obedient to the leading of the Holy Spirit and do what you can with what you have. Do not despise small beginnings.

46

Never Judge a Book by its Cover

But the LORD said to Samuel, "Do not look at his appearance or at his physical stature, because I have refused him. For the LORD does not see as man sees; for man looks at the outward appearance, but the LORD looks at the heart."
1 Samuel 16:7

Joanne and I were working in Bungoma, northern Kenya on the Ugandan border and our visas were about to expire. We decided to go to the border post and have the police stamp our passports to give us an extension. That would be much faster than the long journey to Nairobi to renew the visas.

We set off early one morning. When we reached the border post, we were surprised to see how many trucks were lined up waiting to enter Uganda. I had a narrow path to go through between the trucks and it was tricky manoeuvring our Land Rover and trailer. Unfortunately, I clipped one of the trucks and knocked off a rear mirror. I felt bad about it, but as the driver was nowhere to be seen, I carried on driving.

When I arrived at the Police Station, the Commander

came out to greet me. He looked like a rough chap. He was well-dressed and neatly turned out, but he just looked like he might have an attitude. At that exact moment the irate driver of the vehicle I had damaged, also arrived. I sighed as I thought, "Uh, oh, here's trouble."

"Did you break my rear window mirror?" demanded the truck driver.

"Actually," I responded, "I knocked it. I didn't break the mirror. I kept it. Here it is."

"No," he insisted. "You broke it and now you must pay, or I will call the police."

Joanne and I were the only white people at the border post that day. It was very hot, and the drivers were becoming frustrated with the added delay. We could feel the tension building.

"OK," I said, "How much do you want? Give me an amount."

I only had a few dollars on me, and I was about 2,000 Ugandan shillings short. That is about $5 or R100. The driver was becoming very aggressive, and things were getting ugly. I was also getting hot under the collar myself and I was worried about Joanne's safety.

"I'm sorry, this is all I have got," I said firmly. "What do you want me to do?"

The Station Commander interrupted. "Just calm down everybody," he said. "So, you are short 2000 shillings? I will pay for this man." With that, he took the money out of his pocket and handed it to the driver. We both looked at him in surprise. The driver took the money and left.

I was very grateful and thanked him. "I completely misjudged you," I told him. "I thought you were going to give me a hard time, but you helped us instead. Thank you so much."

He smiled. "I perceive you to be a man of God," he said. "You needed my help. What have you come here for?"

When I told him we had come to have our visas extended, he laughed. "I am the right man for that." "God be with you," he said as he returned our passports.

As we left to return to Bungoma, he shouted after us, "Remember, we are together!"

I prejudged the man because of his rough appearance and was completely misguided. How often do we do that? God does not judge us by our outward appearance either, He looks at our hearts.

Never judge a book by its cover!

47

No One Is Beyond the Reach of Jesus

And they were greatly astonished, saying among themselves, 'Who then can be saved?' But Jesus looked at them and said, "With men it is impossible, but not with God: for with God all things are possible."
Mark 10:26,27

While ministering in Zimbabwe, we were taken to an Old Age Home. It was in a very poor state. The residents were literally starving. When they took me to the storage room, I was heartbroken. There was only one loaf of bread, and it was as hard as a rock. That's all they had to eat. We took all the food supplies in our small land cruiser and left it for them. There wasn't much, but it was all we had.

One of the people accompanying us was a medical doctor. He called me urgently. "Pastor Fergus, you had better come into this room. There is a very ill man here."

I went into the room and saw the man lying naked on a thin sponge mattress. He was emaciated, very thin and weak. He reminded me of photographs I have seen of people coming out of the German concentration camps. "Bring a blanket and cover this man," I said to one of my team.

This man was on his deathbed. Physical food would not help him now, but I had spiritual food that would prepare him for the journey ahead. I could not speak his language. I think he was from Mozambique and probably spoke Portuguese.

I turned to my interpreter who was standing next to me. "Ask him if he is born again or saved."

"He says he doesn't know what that means."

Through the interpreter, I shared the gospel with the dying man. Then I asked him if he wanted to receive the Lord Jesus Christ as his personal Lord and Saviour."

"Yes, I do, sir!" he said through the interpreter.

I knelt next to him, praying for him as he confessed the Lord as his Savior. Before we left the orphanage that day, he passed into the presence of His Saviour. Like the thief on the cross, it's never too late to accept Jesus Christ.

Share the gospel with everyone you can. No one is beyond the reach of Jesus.

48

Patient in Tribulation

But the God of all grace, who called us to His eternal glory by Christ Jesus, after you have suffered a while, perfect, establish, strengthen, and settle you. To Him be the glory and the dominion forever and ever. Amen."
1 Peter 5:10

When we are suffering, we often feel as though our pain will never end. Be encouraged today. The Lord knows exactly where you are and how to minister to you. Do not become despondent. We must be patient in tribulation.

Sometimes you hear about groups going on mission trips. They stay in luxurious hotels, attend conferences in air-conditioned comfort, perhaps speak to a few people, and fly out again. Our missions are nothing like that. Our calling is to reach the unreached in almost inaccessible areas. Over the last twenty-plus years, this ministry has led thousands to the Lord.

We go in groups of three or four. The team sleeps in one little room. All the host family has available may be a bowl of rice and a spoonful of peas and that is your meal for the day. Many times, they have never seen a white man.

We walked into quite a big village in northern Uganda and went from hut to hut, sharing the gospel. Again, we found ourselves having to be patient in tribulation. Drunkards threw beer bottles at us. Local Muslims shouted in anger and threatened to attack us as some of the villagers gave their lives to Jesus. We patiently continued ministering, anointing the sick with oil, and laying hands on them in the name of the Lord Jesus Christ. That village was turned around by the grace of God.

Another time, a group of people attacked us Someone demanded money and when I refused, they became very aggressive. One pushed Joanne over and I prayed for grace. In my BC (before Christ) days, I would have flattened him. She got into the car, and they began beating the team. A young man hit me on the head as we hurriedly packed our equipment in the vehicle. By this time, they were attempting to steal our equipment. Two jumped on the front of the car, another climbed on the roof. We had no fear, but because it looked as though this would develop into a full-scale riot, we jumped in the vehicle and took off at high speed.

When we arrived back at our camp, we broke bread and gave thanks. We were bruised and battered, but no bones were broken. We thanked the Lord for protecting us. I was especially grateful that He kept me from becoming aggressive when my wife was attacked. If I had beaten that man to a pulp, what kind of testimony would that be? We trusted the Lord and He delivered us from evil.

Be patient in tribulation. You are God's Living Bible, the only Bible most people will read!

49

Pilgrims Passing Through

The hope of the righteous will be gladness, but the expectation of the wicked will perish.
Proverbs 10:28

This world is not our home. The Scriptures remind us that we are just strangers and pilgrims passing through on our way to our Eternal Home in Heaven. While we live in this world, it is important to make sure "the world" does not live in us and dominate our lives. *"Beloved, I beg you as sojourners and pilgrims, abstain from fleshly lusts which war against the soul"* (1 Peter 2:11).

As we watch the news, listen to commentaries, and read the newspapers, it seems to be all doom and gloom, especially for born-again believers as persecution increases in these last days. Wickedness and evil people seem to be taking control of the nations and things are going from bad to worse.

The Psalmist became very discouraged when he saw the wickedness around him. He said, "My steps had nearly slipped. For I was envious of the boastful, when I saw the prosperity of the wicked... Pride serves as their necklace, violence covers them like a garment. Their eyes bulge with abundance. They have more than their heart could wish. They scoff and speak wickedly concerning oppression. They speak loftily. They set their mouth against the heavens, and their tongue walks through the earth" (Psalm 73:1-12).

He stopped looking around and looked up, which made him realise their arrogance and boasting was simply pure propaganda. "It was too painful for me," he wrote. "Until I went into the sanctuary of God; Then I understood their end. Surely you set them in slippery places... in a moment they are utterly consumed with terrors" (Psalm 73:16-19).

It does not end well for the wicked and the unbeliever. It ends very badly according to the last book of the Bible. They are on a slippery slope to Hell. Death for them means an eternity of terror.

For the believer, death is the doorway to an eternity with the Lord. A new trip to a new country and a new land to be with the Lord Jesus Christ. We have nothing to fear. We are on the winning side because we chose Jesus. We believe every word written in the Word of God. The hope of the righteous will be gladness.

In these difficult days, keep focused on the Lord. *"You will keep him in perfect peace, whose mind is stayed on You, because he trusts in You"* (Isaiah 26:3).

50

Pilgrims Passing Through

Wine is a mocker, Strong drink is a brawler, and whoever is led astray by it is not wise.
Proverbs 20:1

Many years ago, I had just come back from Germany and was working with my brother, Angus, in Greytown. The Lord was preparing me to fulfil my call to become a full-time Missionary. One day He taught me a valuable lesson.

I used to enjoy a nice cold beer with Joanne on occasion because it gets very hot in KwaZulu-Natal. Coming from Germany, where beer is like drinking *Coca-Cola*, it wasn't considered an issue. I don't judge people who enjoy a glass of wine or a cold beer, but something happened to me that shocked me to the core and changed my lifestyle.

One Friday afternoon, Joanne and I went shopping in town. "We don't have any cold beers for tonight. Do you want to go to the store and get some?" she asked.

Off I went to the bottle store and bought some cold beers. A young man came up behind me holding a crate of beer. He also had bottles of brandy and whiskey. The young girl serving at the counter smiled at him.

"Wow," she laughed, "you sure are going to have a party this weekend."

"Oh no," he replied. "I'm going to drink all of this. And I'm going to get as drunk as I possibly can."

I was shocked by his reaction to her.

I wanted to say, "You know, you shouldn't be doing that, son."

I looked at him and he looked back at me. Both of us were silent. I had no words because I was acutely aware there were beers in my own hand. How could I counsel him? He doesn't know I only occasionally drink beer and sometimes only shandies at night (a beer cocktail made of beer and citrusy lemon-lime soda). How can I tell him to stop drinking while he looks at the alcohol I am carrying? What kind of Christian leader says one thing and does another? I was thoroughly convicted by the Holy Spirit that day to be a genuine example of the believer.

Subdued, I went home and discussed it with Joanne. That was a wake-up call for us. It's easy to talk the walk, but it's not so easy to walk the walk. It was a very long time ago and Joanne and I still don't touch alcohol to this day.

We must practice what we preach to be effective witnesses for the Lord.

Is there something the Lord is speaking to you about?

51

Pray Always

Then you will walk safely in your way, And your foot will not stumble. When you lie down, you will not be afraid; Yes, you will lie down and your sleep will be sweet. Do not be afraid of sudden terror, Nor of trouble from the wicked when it comes; For the LORD will be your confidence, And will keep your foot from being caught.
Proverbs 3:23-26

We were in Juba, Sudan. We had quite a distance to travel that day to minister to a group waiting for us. David and I broke bread and prayed together before we left. We asked the Lord to protect us and give us favour with the people as we shared the Gospel. Our driver was waiting downstairs. He greeted us and we set off immediately for our destination.

"Wait," I said firmly. "Stop the car!"

"Have you forgotten something, Doctor?" he asked in surprise.

"We haven't prayed for travelling mercies," I said.

We prayed for travelling mercies. We prayed for our driver. We had a long journey ahead over very rough roads, so we prayed about the car itself, the wheels, and the engine. We always do that on all our trips. And so, we set off.

We were about to turn onto a dirt road when we saw a 20-seater bus approaching. It was followed by a 12-seater taxi travelling at enormous speed. The taxi driver tried to overtake the bus and came onto our side of the road. When he realized he couldn't pass the bus, he backed off but misjudged and hit the side of the bus. The bus went into a spin. The taxi came straight at us. At the last minute, the driver turned his wheel and careered down a steep embankment. The taxi went straight through the bushes and trees. The bus stopped and the angry passengers ran down the embankment and beat up the driver. Fortunately, the police arrived and arrested him.

We were in shock as we continued to travel to our meeting. About one thousand people were already waiting and soon another large crowd arrived to join them. 72 people gave their lives to Jesus that day. I also met an important leader. He arrived at the meeting with his bodyguards and stopped to talk with me afterwards. He is a man of influence and a very humble Christian.

The Lord spared us from a head-on collision and the devil's plans to involve us in that accident came to nothing.

When you travel, always be sure to pray first, even if you are just going to your local shop. You never know what is happening in the spiritual realm.

52

Put On the Whole Armour of God

Finally, my brethren, be strong in the Lord and in the power of His might. Put on the whole armor of God, that you may be able to stand against the wiles of the devil.
Ephesians 10:10,11

I have walked with the Lord Jesus Christ for many years and have come to know that the devil is a bully. He comes against the children of God in every way he can. He's a master at stirring up fear and unbelief and knows how to make trouble. He's been doing this for a very long time. He comes against our families, health, finances, business, and relationships. We are living in the Last Days and the devil knows his time is short. Be sure, he will come at us with all he's got and turn up the heat.

The Bible says we must resist him in the power of the Lord. That is the only way to handle bullies. *"Therefore submit to God. Resist the devil and he will flee from you"* (James 4:7). Why will he flee? The Word says, *"… because He who is in you is greater than he who is in the world"* (1 John 4:4). If we are walking closely with the Lord, we can take whatever comes our way in His strength. Make a firm decision to be strong in the Lord. Don't give an inch, dig your heels in, no matter what comes your way. If you know the Lord Jesus Christ and you are filled with the Holy Spirit, you can face anything. We have been in dangerous places on the mission field. Our teams have faced hardship, terrorists, demon-possessed people, and much more. The Lord has always been true to His Word and given us the strength to stand firm and keep going.

Of course, we must do our part. *"Therefore, put on every piece of God's armor so you will be able to resist the enemy in the time of evil. Then after the battle you will still be standing firm. Stand your ground, putting on the belt of truth and the body armor of God's righteousness. For shoes, put on the peace that comes from the Good News so that you will be fully prepared. In addition to all of these, hold up the shield of faith to stop the fiery arrows of the devil. Put on salvation as your helmet, and take the sword of the Spirit, which is the Word of God. Pray in the Spirit at all times and on every occasion. Stay alert and be persistent in your prayers for all believers everywhere"*
Ephesians 10:11-18 NLT).

Pray about everything. Pray for one another. Pray for your family. Break bread regularly. Plead the Blood of the Lamb over your family, your friends, your church, your relationships, and your business. Read the Bible daily and spend time with the Lord and His people.

53

Ready In Season and Out of Season

Preach the word! Be ready in season and out of season. Convince, rebuke, exhort, with all longsuffering and teaching.
2 Timothy 4:2

Experiences in life have prepared us to share the gospel in every season. Growing up in Central Africa exposed me to many experiences that prepared me for ministry in later life. I grew up in Northern Rhodesia, now called Zambia. My mom would often take us shopping in the little stores nearby. We were used to mothers breastfeeding their children under the trees. It was perfectly natural for us to see little naked children running around.

When I was ministering in Southern Sudan during July 2023, we visited an area about ten kilometres out of Juba, right on the banks of the River Nile. We left early in the morning and drove down dusty roads until we found a group of people we could minister to. Nearly all of them were stark naked.

The heat in the Sudan is extreme. Annual temperatures range between 36 and 42 degrees C, with summer temperatures often exceeding 46 degrees. Apparently, the Nile crocodiles don't usually come this far down the river, so the people gather there to fish, swim, and do their washing, Now it's one thing seeing a naked child but it comes as something of a shock for Westerners to see men and women, young and old totally naked.

How I thank the Lord He prepared me for this moment. Their nakedness did not concern me for one moment. David and Butrus were locals, so they were not perturbed either. All we saw were men, women, and children who needed to hear about Jesus.

When we stopped the car, they all looked at us. They were not embarrassed, and neither were we. "This Man of God has come from London. He is a Pastor. Do you want him to pray for you?" shouted Butrus. "Yes," they shouted enthusiastically. I shared the gospel of Jesus Christ and prayed with those who wished to repent and give their lives to Jesus. Many gave their lives to Christ, and we prayed for peace in their war-torn country.

We went back to the car and crossed the river. On the other side of the Nile River more people were busy with their daily tasks. They listened intently as we shared the gospel, and many responded. It reminded me of the scripture recorded in Genesis 2:25 about Adam and Eve. *"And they were both naked, the man and his wife, and were not ashamed."* These people were not ashamed, and neither were we. What joy we experienced as they gave their lives to Jesus.

May I encourage you to share the gospel with someone today? Do not be put off by their clothes, status in society, or the size of their home. The Lord has already prepared you to be a witness for Him in season and out of season.

54
Righteous Anger

Be angry, and do not sin: do not let the sun go down on your wrath, nor give place to the devil.
Ephesians 4:26

There are times when you must accept injustice, but there are also times when you must act to resolve issues. The important thing is to act without uncontrolled anger, resentment, and bitterness. We may be angry but must not sin in our response.

When we were still based on our Mission Station in KwaZula-Natal, South Africa, one of our senior staff members came running to the house. "Sir," he said breathlessly, "there are people on your property, and they are stealing your cattle troughs.

I had three expensive, heavy, steel water troughs. Thieves were constantly on the lookout for anything made of metal. They made good money selling metal to scrap dealers illegally. I jumped in my land cruiser and rushed to the bottom end of the farm. By this time, they were well on their way with my troughs in the back of their *bakkie* (small lorry).

From experience, I knew which way they would go so I

chased after them. I found them at a local scrap metal dealer. They were waiting in a queue while the metal was being weighed. Yes, I was angry and, yes, I was determined to get my equipment back. But I was not in an uncontrollable rage by the grace of God. *"For the [resentful, deep-seated] anger of man does not produce the righteousness of God [that standard of behaviour which He requires from us]"* (James 1:20 Amplified Bible).

When I got out of my vehicle, the three thieves looked at me in shock. I put my hand in the window and took the keys. "I am arresting you for theft," I said firmly. The Moslem owner of the business came running towards us. "What do you think you are doing?" he shouted. "I am the owner of this place, and you are on my property. Stop harassing my clients."

"Your clients are thieves," I said firmly. "They have just stolen these troughs from my farm in Hermannsburg."

"So, what proof do you have?" he responded.

My cattleman answered, "I am the proof. I saw them."

"Any more trouble from you," I told him, "And I will arrest you for buying stolen goods."

Joanne had called the police in the meantime, and they arrived at that moment. We put the cattle troughs in my pickup while the police arrested the three thieves. I realised they could have attacked us on the road as we chased after them. I thanked the Lord for His Hand of protection on us and forgave them. Things could have turned out very differently if I had given way to rage and lost control of my temper.

"You used to do these things when your life was still part of this world. But now is the time to get rid of anger, rage, malicious behavior, slander, and dirty language. Don't lie to each other, for you have stripped off your old sinful nature and all its wicked deeds. Put on your new nature, and be renewed as you learn to know your Creator and become like Him" (Colossians 3:7-10 NLT).

55

Seasons In Our Lives

To everything there is a season, A time for every purpose under heaven.
Ecclesiastes 3:1

Joanne and I went for a walk in this iconic city of London where we are now living. The seasons were changing. The leaves of the trees were falling, and we were fascinated with their lovely yellow-orange colours. Autumn is a beautiful time in the UK.

It reminded me that we have seasons in our lives as well. Everything we experience as we go through our seasons has a purpose. When we go through seasons of despair, discouragement, hurt, pain, and sickness, we often wonder if the season will ever end. Take courage and learn from nature that when one season passes, a new season comes. Autumn turns into winter, winter into spring, and spring into summer.

"While the earth remains, Seedtime and harvest, Cold and heat, Winter and summer, And day and night shall not cease" (Genesis 8:22).

That mighty man of God, Charles Haddon Spurgeon, wrote this about seasons: "The seasons change, and you change, but your Lord abides evermore the same, and the streams of His love are as deep, as broad, and as full as ever."

He also wrote: "So in the spiritual kingdom, in the life of the believer, and in the history of the church of God, all things are made to work for good, and the spiritual is being educated into the heavenly. In our seasons there is an order visible to God, even when we walk in darkness and see no light."

No matter how this last week has treated you, Monday is a new start to a new week. Next month is a new month, and next year is a new year. Don't look back. Be encouraged, Seasons come, and seasons go but we serve a God who is the same yesterday, today, and forever. He knows what we go through and how to sustain us in all our seasons. "Through the Lord's mercies we are not consumed, because His compassions fail not. They are new every morning; Great is Your faithfulness" (Lamentations 3:22-23).

So be encouraged. Whatever season you're in, it will pass. "Weeping may endure for a night, but joy comes in the morning" (Psalm 30:5).

It is always interesting to hear what people have said as their season on earth ended and they departed this life. The last recorded words of the Lord Jesus Christ are found in the last chapter of the last book of the Bible. "He who testifies to these things says, 'Surely I am coming quickly.' Amen. Even so, come, Lord Jesus!" (Revelation 22:20).

That is one season we can really look forward to – the soon return of our Lord Jesus Christ.

56

Senders and Goers

But you will receive power and ability when the Holy Spirit comes upon you; and you will be My witnesses [to tell people about Me] both in Jerusalem and in all Judea, and Samaria, and even to the ends of the earth.
Acts 1:8 Amplified Bible (AMP)

There are two kinds of people that make missionary work possible to the ends of the earth – the senders and the goers. Neither group is more important than the other. Each has a vital role to play in mission work and will receive their reward from the Lord Himself. Not everyone is called to be a missionary, but all Christians are called to share the Gospel, empowered by the Holy Spirit.

The senders play a vital role. They make it possible for missionaries to physically go into areas as the Lord leads them. Senders pray and encourage missionaries. We never left our mission station without the whole team praying over the Landrovers, trucks, and missionaries. It is so encouraging to know they continue in prayer while we are away.

Senders provide resources and equipment. The gospel

is free but the means to share it involves expense. We must put diesel in our trucks, pay border fees, accommodation, medicines, and food. Bibles in the local language are needed, as well as other supplies. Messiah Ministries International never asks for money. We trust the Lord to send those who will support us in prayer and by practical means.

George Mueller is a great example for us. He never asked for finance as he opened those big orphanages in Bristol and fed thousands of children by faith. He just obeyed the Lord's leading and did the job he was called to do.

The Lord's command is to go into the world and preach the Gospel right to the ends of the earth. Senders do that by supporting missionaries. T.L. Osborne, a world-renowned evangelist, said a church that is not mission-oriented is a dead church. Christians must take missions very seriously.

The missionaries are goers. We are the ones who physically go out and minister to the lost. Many of the people we go to in rural areas don't have networks. They don't have televisions and other forms of communication. Missionaries must come to where they are, preach the gospel, minister to the sick, make disciples, and plant churches.

Missionary work is not an easy ministry. We try to live with the people. I've slept in basic thatched huts, on the floor, and under trees. I vividly remember waking up one morning covered with ticks. There are rats and snakes. You wash and shave out of half a bucket of water, but the people see your heart. There are no video cameras, no money, and no glory. Just malaria, tick-bite fever, beatings, and being stoned by unbelievers.

Our teams have suffered all these things. But they fade into insignificance when you see these precious people transformed by the Gospel. As Paul wrote, "I planted, Apollos watered, and God gave the increase" (1 Corinthians 3:6).

Senders and Goers share the reward. Which one are you?

57

Servants on Assignment

Do all things without complaining and disputing, that you may become blameless and harmless, children of God without fault in the midst of a crooked and perverse generation, among whom you shine as lights in the world.
Philippians 2:14

When the Lord healed me of cancer, I promised to serve Him for the rest of my life. We sold up and left Germany to move to South Africa to work with Angus. I thought Angus and I were going to change the world and couldn't wait to get going.

We arrived on his farm, and I was ready for action. One week later, Angus 'phoned me. There were two elderly widows living on the farm, Peggy O'Neill and Moira Mathieson and they had a problem.

"Fergus," he said, "Moira's sink is blocked. Can you go and have a look at it?"

A little Zulu boy named Lucky came with me. The drain was completely blocked so I used a shifting spanner to release the nut on the downpipe into the drain.

Remember, this successful, professional golfer had just come from Germany. Golfers always dress well, and I was wearing very smart jeans, a brand-new shirt, and expensive shoes.

As I released the nut, all Moira's cooking for the past weeks shot out of the pipe and covered me from head to toe. I wasn't very impressed. I didn't say anything at the time because I was a Christian now and didn't swear anymore.

I finished the job, refused tea, and sulked all the way home. When I saw Joanne, I exploded. "I'm here to preach the Gospel, not fix motors and blocked sinks. Just look at my clothes," I complained.

"Wait a minute, Fergus!" my dear wife said. "Didn't you make a covenant with the Lord in Germany and promise to serve Him? You just served Him by helping a widow clear a blocked kitchen sink!"

I learned a big lesson that day. Ministry is not always about the big crusades or missions in remote jungles. Day-to-day things are also very important to the Lord and He requires that we do all things without complaining and disputing.

"So you too, when you have done everything that was assigned and commanded you, say, 'We are unworthy servants [undeserving of praise or a reward, for we have not gone beyond our obligation]; we have merely done what we ought to do" (Luke17i:10).

58

Stay In Your Lane

Then the twelve summoned the multitude of the disciples and said, "It is not desirable that we should leave the word of God and serve tables. Therefore, brethren, seek out from among you seven men of good reputation, full of the Holy Spirit and wisdom, whom we may appoint over this business; but we will give ourselves continually to prayer and to the ministry of the word.
Acts 6:2-4

I was a Golf Professional when God called me to be an Evangelist. I learned the hard way how important it is to stay in your appointed lane and serve God in what you have been called to do.

After working with my brother, Angus Buchan, in Shalom Ministries for five years, our seasons changed. My son, Fraser, and I felt called to fulltime missionary work in Central Africa. I decided it would be wise to establish a base in South Africa where we could raise some livestock and grow cabbages and maize. I bought a smallholding in Hermannsburg, KwaZulu-Natal.

It would be our base camp and mission station from where we could also minister to the Zulu people. Soon we had 82 heads of cattle and thousands of chickens. Life was very busy. But raising livestock was not what God called me to do. I was not anointed to be a farmer and problems soon began to surface. Ministry began to take second place and I was becoming very frustrated. I asked the Lord for wisdom. His answer came quickly.

When a chicken sneezes, it means it's got flu and can die within hours. I rushed to the local vet for medication to put in their water. A board in the doorway stopped the chickens running out and I tripped over it. There is nothing like the smell of chicken manure and I fell into a massive pile headfirst, still managing to save the expensive medication! Joanne and the staff laughed until tears ran down their faces. I was miserable. I can still smell that manure.

"Lord," I cried out. "I can't do this anymore. Please help me! I repent."

We put the smallholding on the market. Local people advised us to cut our losses and run but God heard our prayers and sent us a buyer. He remains faithful to His Word even when we fail. I had good intentions and worked hard, but I learned God's wisdom is best. It is not desirable to leave the Word of God and serve tables. We must stay in our lane and not become distracted. My calling is to preach the Gospel and reach the lost. God used chicken manure to impress that on me.

What is He saying to you? Are you fully committed to the task the Lord has given you?

59

Stefan and Theresa, Soldiers of the Cross

By faith Abraham obeyed when he was called to go out to the place which we would receive as an inheritance. And he went out, not knowing where he was going.
Hebrews 11:8

On our first trip to Australia, Fraser and I met a young couple named Stefan and Theresa. It was a divine appointment. We were invited by the Bushney brothers, George and Alistair, who were living in Perth. Our first meeting was a men's breakfast. It was well-supported.

I was sitting at a table, waiting for the meeting to start when a very big guy sat down next to me. "Hello, mate," he said. "My name is Stefan." We chatted for a while until I was introduced as the guest speaker. After ministering the Word, I was led to pray for people struggling with alcohol issues. That is a big problem in Australia. As I invited people to come forward for prayer, I saw Stefan get up and walk towards me.

After the meeting, Stefan thanked me. "I heard someone named Buchan was speaking at the meeting. When I sat down at your table, I didn't know who you were. In fact, I shouldn't even have been at that table." He was delivered that morning from his addiction to alcohol.

We had another eight or nine meetings planned so I invited Stefan and his lovely wife, Theresa, to attend. They came every night. Theresa worked as a PA for a very wealthy businessman in Australia. Stefan was a Cordon Bleu chef and they lived in a beautiful mansion. We became very good friends.

"Can we come to Africa and do some mission work with you," they asked. I agreed and they came on two mission outreaches. By the time they returned home, Stefan and Theresa were growing strong in the Lord.

Later they contacted me. "We feel led to sell up and go to Cambodia," they said. "We want to open an orphanage there." And that is what they did. The Lord Jesus said, *"Go therefore and make disciples of all the nations"* (Matthew 28:18). Some hear, but never go. Others go, but soon give up. Stefan and Theresa followed through.

Nearly three years ago, I received an email from Theresa. "Stefan suffered a massive heart attack and has died," she wrote. Stefan is the first Australian missionary to be buried in that area of Cambodia.

Theresa is determined to finish the race. She made the decision to remain in Cambodia and continue to take care of the orphans. That is commitment.

May the words of this old hymn inspire and challenge you.

> *There's a work for Jesus, ready at your hand,*
> *'Tis a task the Master just for you has planned.*
> *Haste to do His bidding, yield Him service true;*

There's a work for Jesus none but you can do.
Refrain:
Work for Jesus, day by day,
Serve Him ever, falter never; Christ obey.
Yield Him service loyal, true,
There's a work for Jesus none but you can do.

There's a work for Jesus, humble though it be,
'Tis the very service He would ask of thee.
Go where fields are whitened, and the lab'rers few;
There's a work for Jesus none but you can do.

There's a work for Jesus, precious souls to bring,
Tell them of His mercies, tell them of your King.
Faint not, nor grow weary, He will strength renew;
There's a work for Jesus none but you can do.

© Elsie D. Yale, 1912

60

Supplying and Essential Service

Brethren, of anyone among you wanders from the truth, and someone turns him back, let him know that he who turns a sinner from the error of his way will save a soul from death and cover a multitude of sins.
James 5:19,20

When we walk in the streets of London, looking for people to introduce to the Lord Jesus Christ, we are often stopped by police. That was especially so during the lockdown time when the streets were deserted, except for the homeless people.

"What are you doing here? Who gave you permission?" they challenge us. I always carry my Pastor's Certificate and I tell them, "I'm supplying an essential service. I'm praying for the homeless, for peace and security, and for their salvation."

They always look surprised when I follow up with, "Can I pray for you?" Some refuse but many say yes. We have prayed for many policemen and women, paramedics, and other essential service people. Some we have led to the Lord. They have a difficult job to do and thank us for taking the time to minister to them. We love doing it. London's streets are back to normal and very busy. It grieves us to see how people often just walk past these hopeless people as if they are invisible. Some look at them with disdain and disgust. Joanne and I were in Victoria Station one morning. We watched as a well-dressed woman threw a pound note at a homeless lady as if she was throwing a piece of meat at a dog. That touched us deeply and we stopped to talk to the homeless woman. We were overjoyed to be able to lead her to personal faith in the Lord Jesus Christ.

We usually walk the streets for about two hours on Saturday mornings and it is the highlight of my life. We have been privileged to lead hundreds of these forgotten people to the Lord. Before we leave them, we always tell them that we love them. Their response is usually, "We love you too." They hug us and shake our hands. By the time we get home, our clothes are permeated with the smell of unwashed bodies, but it does not offend us at all. That's what Jesus did.

The most important thing for us is that the smell of sin no longer lingers in their lives. Souls are saved from eternal death, and a multitude of sins are washed away. Future sins and evil deeds they may have committed as unregenerate sinners may never happen.

Think again when you pass the homeless. Peter said, *"Silver and gold I do not have, but what I do have I give you: In the name of Jesus Christ of Nazareth, rise up and walk"* (Acts 3:6).

We are supplying an essential service on behalf of the Lord.

61

Take Up Your Cross and Follow Jesus

He who loves father or mother more than Me is not worthy of Me. And he who loves son or daughter more than Me is not worthy of Me. And he who does not take his cross and follow after Me is not worthy of Me.
Matthew 10:37-38

After I was healed of cancer, I had to keep my part of the covenant. That meant I had to leave Germany and serve the Lord as a full-time missionary. To my surprise, when I broke the news to our twin daughters, Sheena and Kirsty, they were not impressed. They were both living in Germany and had become German citizens. I just assumed they would travel back to Africa with Joanne and myself. Fraser was already working with Angus, and we planned to join them.

"No," they insisted. "We don't want to go back to Africa. We are not Africans anymore. We are now Europeans with German passports. Our work is here."

Our hearts were broken, as you can imagine. We had left Africa without little Alistair. We looked forward to meeting up with Fraser at Shalom, but now our family was splitting again. We love our girls and the thought of leaving them behind was very difficult for both of us. Jesus' challenge to take up our cross and follow Him is very powerful. I've preached on this scripture many times, but how differently you feel things when they come to your door and your home. I'll never forget that day at Nuremberg Airport. When the girls came to see us off, Joanne and I were heartbroken because we had made our choice and there was no going back. At the time, it was a very difficult decision to leave our twins behind.

Yes, we were going back to South Africa to meet up with Fraser again. This was to be the start of our ministry journey and the fulfilment of our call. But it came at great cost.

Was it worth it? Abundantly, yes! Taking up our cross and following Jesus has led us on the most amazing journey. We have seen literally thousands of people from all walks of life come into the Kingdom of God. We have experienced miracles and walked with the Lord Jesus through many ups and downs. Eventually, the Lord led us to establish our Mission Headquarters in London. Sheena now stays with us, and Kirsty lives just down the road. Fraser is married to Marta, and they live in the United States.

It is easy to say, "When we have made enough money," or "when we retire," or whatever your "when we" might be, then you will follow the call of God in your life. The Lord is challenging you today to take up your cross now and follow Him. Are you ready to go out on a limb for the Lord Jesus? It may not be an easy decision, but you will never regret deciding to follow Jesus.

62

The Christian's Commission

*He sent them to preach the Kingdom of God
and to heal the sick.*
Luke 9:2

We were in northern Uganda, hundreds of kilometres from Kampala as we walked into a village marketplace. It was quite a large village and there were a lot of people milling around. We built a small platform out of sand and that is where I preached from. There was a bar close by and some young men drinking beer started heckling me. I'm used to that kind of environment, so I kept preaching. After praying with those who wanted to receive Christ, I said we were going to pray for the sick. In our ministry, we believe in laying hands on the sick and anointing them with oil in the Name of the Lord Jesus Christ.

It's customary in that part of the world for people to kneel when they are praying. I moved among the people, anointing them with oil, laying hands on them, and praying the prayer of faith. Among them was a woman in a beautiful, brightly coloured dress wearing a lovely matching head covering. I put my hand on her head, and said, "Be healed, in the Name of Jesus!" Someone called me. "I have problems in my stomach and believe I have cancer," she said as I prayed for her. There were so many people requesting prayer, that it was very late when we finished the meeting.

The next morning, a group of Pastors woke me. They were very excited. "There are two women here you must speak to," they said. I went outside and there were the two women I remembered praying for the previous day.

The lady with the matching dress and head covering spoke first. "Sir," she said, you prayed for me yesterday. You never asked me what to pray for, and I want to tell you what happened to me." It turned out that she had a massive open tumour on her head, covered by the headdress. The Lord Jesus Christ completely healed her. That night before she went to bed, she had a bath and as she was washing her head the whole tumour came away in her hands.

I looked at the elderly second woman. "You are the one who had the stomach problem," I said. "You said you had cancer." She smiled at me. "Yes, I did have cancer. But I am here to testify that the cancer is no more."

"How do you know you are healed?" I asked her.

"After you prayed for me, I went back to my house and got ready for bed. I went to the bathroom," she said, "and everything bad in my stomach came out. It wasn't like any normal bowel movement. This morning when I awoke, I was completely healed and free of pain."

"Please come back to the village before you leave. My son is the mayor. I want to tell everyone what happened," she insisted. We went back and the whole village responded to the Gospel message and surrendered their lives to Christ. One miracle is indeed worth a thousand sermons.

God wants all His people to operate in the supernatural Gifts of the Spirit. The Lord can use you to win the lost and heal the sick in your neighbourhood. Are you available?

63

The Christian's Commission

But I am poor and needy; Yet the LORD thinks upon me.
You are my help and my deliverer;
Do not delay, O my God.
Psalm 40:17

It was our second year on the Mission Station in KwaZulu-Natal. Fraser and I were chatting, and he said, "Dad, there are so many orphans in the valley because of AIDS, what about us hosting a Christmas party for them?" Joanne and I agreed we could do that.

We started to work on the logistics. Our large open shed easily catered for the anticipated three hundred children, all poor and needy. A large store in Greytown came on board with frozen packets of chicken thighs and chicken breasts. They also gave us a lot of mielie meal (maize) and some curry powder.

We started cooking on Christmas eve. Joanne's mother was visiting us for Christmas, and she helped in the kitchen. As you can imagine, we had massive pots going to cook all that food. Cabbages grew in abundance on the farm, so we made curried cabbage as well, which the Zulu people love.

Christmas Day dawned bright and sunny. The Lord kindly sent us helpers. Two friends from East London, John and Minnie Lambie, and a German couple from the Hermannsburg Station joined us on Christmas Day and helped us set up the food on the tables. Jo's mom and brother, Peter, who was visiting from Canada also were a great help in setting up and serving. We gave the children paper plates, and they lined up enthusiastically for their dinner.

After giving thanks, they got stuck into their meal. Each child received a large portion of mielie meal, a big chicken piece, curried cabbage and sauce, with a chocolate bar to round off the meal. They loved it. The big moment for them, of course, was their Christmas gift. Every child received a gift, and they went home with big smiles.

The party lasted about five hours. After we cleaned up, the exhausted team sat down for our Christmas Day meal, which we had also precooked. It was still very hot, and we sat on the veranda, eating, and chatting.

John turned to me quietly. "Fergus," he said, "I am a Scotsman from Glasgow, but this is the best Christmas I have ever had in my entire life." Peter also said it was the most rewarding Christmas he had experienced. John wasn't a professing Christian at the time, but when he died a few years later and I conducted his funeral service, I am happy to say he was totally committed to the Lord Jesus.

I think it is still probably the greatest Christmas I've ever had. The Lord said it is better to give than to receive, and we were certainly blessed that day. It was a Christmas we will never forget.

Does this story inspire you to bless somebody who could never pay you back? Go ahead, do it. You will never be sorry.

64

The Desires of Your Heart

But seek first the kingdom of God and His righteousness, and all these things shall be added to you.
Matthew 6:33

I had two special desires in my heart, and both were fulfilled by the Lord as I focused on fulfilling my call to share the Gospel.

My first desire came to pass when I was ministering in Kenya. I have ministered in many countries of the world, but I longed to move out of stadiums, halls, and churches. I strongly desired to preach the gospel under the trees to rural people. An opportunity suddenly opened to minister to the Maasai tribe, and we drove down to Maasai land, an area of about 600,000 square hectares. The Maasai are t tall people. An average Maasai man is about six-foot-five tall.

The host pastor took me to the Maasai Mara national game reserve, locally known simply as The Mara. It is situated in Narok, Kenya, Here I preached under a thornbush tree. Just a stone's throw away, giraffes walked past on one side. On the other side, a group of monkeys sauntered by. The Maasai have no fear of animals. The animals fear the Maasai warriors. Even lions run from them.

They started getting excited as they heard the Word of God. What a privilege it was to preach to these delightful people. People from Western countries show their excitement by clapping their hands or raising their arms. The Maasai drop their arms to their side and jump nearly half a meter off the ground. It was a wonderful experience. Over 200 Maasai accepted the Lord that day. Since then, I've been in many rural places in Africa, including the vast Congo jungle. It is one of the delights of my life.

My second desire was totally the opposite. I longed to preach to my own people in northeast Scotland, known as the Highlands. My good friends, James and Marie Sutherland, invited me to preach in one of the churches in the county of Buchan. About 300 people came, which is a good turnout for Scotland, and many of them responded to the altar call.

When I went to the door to greet the people as they left, it seemed everybody was a Buchan. I met Jimmy Buchan, Johnny Buchan, Billy Buchan, Rory Buchan, Sue Buchan, Janie Buchan, and Bonnie Buchan. An elderly lady addressed me as "Laddie" (a term of endearment). "It was a blessing today to have a Buchan preaching to the Buchans," she said as she shook my hand. She must have been in the 90s. What joy I had that day.

Two desires, worlds apart, were literally fulfilled for me – preaching under thorn trees to the Maasai and preaching to my own people in Bonny Scotland.

What are your deepest desires? Seek first the kingdom of God and His righteousness, and all these things will be added unto you.

65

The Faithfulness of God

*May He send you help from the sanctuary,
And strengthen you out of Zion.*
Psalm 20:2

This story took place many years ago when Angus and I were two young men living just outside Kitwe in Zambia. I was about 19-years-old at the time. I had gone to my golf club in *Nchanga* and Angus went shopping. As he was driving towards the local shops, Angus saw a family stranded on the side of the road. He stopped to help. "It looks like my water pump is broken," the driver said. "I need to get to *Nchanga*." Angus towed the car all the way to their home in *Nchanga*, about thirty kilometres away, and then drove back to do his shopping and go home.

It is a small world. This man later became my caddy. His name is Bob Hayward. I was the only golfer in Zambia with a white caddy and we became good friends. He had a young son named Robert. Eventually the Haywards moved to Zimbabwe (then known as Rhodesia).

Many years later, Fraser was ministering in Zimbabwe.

He was stranded in the early hours of the morning in a very unsafe area. Suddenly a motor car stopped, and a man got out. "Have you got a problem, son?" he asked. "Yes, sir," said Fraser. "I have a flat and no spanners to remove the nuts."

"I don't have any either," he said. "I will go back to my farm and get some tools." He returned, changed the wheel, and invited Fraser to his farm. He repaired the damaged tyre and Fraser was very thankful.

"What's your name, son?" the man asked. When Fraser told him his name, his face lit up. "I know your father, Fergus Buchan. We are good friends. My name is Bob Hayward. I've met your uncle too, Angus Buchan. He helped me many years ago when I was stranded on the road. It is only a privilege and an honour to help you." Bob and his wife brought out tea and sandwiches and saw Fraser off on his journey back to South Africa.

Many times, good deeds go unnoticed by fellow human beings, but the Lord never forgets your acts of kindness. Even a cup of cold water given in His Name will have its reward. Help really does come from the sanctuary.

Never get tired of doing good things for people. *"But do not forget to do good and to share, for such sacrifices God is well pleased"* (Hebrews 13:16).

66

The God of the Impossible

Do not let your heart faint, do not be afraid, and do not tremble or be terrified because of them; for the LORD your God is He who goes with you, to fight for you against your enemies, to save you.
Deuteronomy 20:5

How do you handle disappointments? How do you react to loss? Maybe you applied for a position and didn't get it? Or put in a tender for a business deal and was unsuccessful? Perhaps you've walked a long road with somebody, and they've let you down. How do you cope with that?

Before I went into full-time ministry, I used to be a golf professional and played all over the world. It took hard practice to prepare for tournaments. On the first day, you would always find me on the green bright and early, warming up and ready for a great day.

There were days when I would hit that golf ball straight and true, right onto the first tee, and then play badly the whole round. Even the second round was miserable, and I'd miss the cut. Such disappointment!

What did I do? Throw my clubs in the water? Pack up playing golf? No, I had to go back to the practice green and work on my game again. The famous golfer, Gary Player, said, "The harder I practise, the luckier I get." That great Mexican champion, Lee Trevino, said, "You've got to learn to lose first before you can win."

That is how life is. We must give it all we have. Never give up. If you are a cowboy and fall off your horse, get up, dust yourself down, and get back on that horse.

The Word of God encourages us to trust in the Lord when we suffer defeat or feel we have lost out. He does with you to fight for you against your enemies and to save and guide you. Let us learn from our mistakes and not repeat them.

You may be in a seemingly impossible situation. It may be in your marriage or your business. It could be in your church, your relationships, or your family. Keep your eyes on the Lord Jesus and not your situation. Things that seem out of control to us, are never beyond the Lord's control. "But Jesus looked at them [His disciples] and said, 'With men it is impossible, but not with God; for with God all things are possible.'"

Jeremiah prayed, *"Ah, Lord God! Behold, You have made the heavens and the earth by Your great power and outstretched arm. There is nothing too hard for you"* (Jeremiah 32:17

Do not give up. Be strong. Be faithful. You may lose a few battles, but that doesn't mean you will lose the war. Keep your eyes on the Lord Jesus and watch the God of the Impossible make impossible things possible.

67

The Lord's Protection

Many are the afflictions of the righteous, But the LORD delivers him out of them all. He guards all his bones; Not one of them is broke.
Psalms 34:19-20

The protection of the Lord is very important, not just on the mission field but also in our everyday lives. Whether you are a pastor, a mom, or a dad, and you go to work every day, or travel, things can happen in a split second.

We were in a town called Bungoma on the Uganda border, travelling down one of the main roads when we were caught in a traffic jam. This is not a particularly busy road, so we were surprised to see so many cars backed up.

There was a lot of shouting, and we heard a riot was taking place. It seems somebody had been caught stealing fish and was shot. We could hear more gunfire as we waited. A big mob rushed towards us, and I saw a man with a half brick in his hands. He was aiming it right at my head. I closed my eyes, and held up my hands in a praying position, waiting for the windscreen to explode. Afterwards I heard that five or six men were trying to pull Joanne out of the car at the same time. Bishop Fred was sitting in the back, praying. There was silence and when I opened my eyes, all the assailants were gone.

By this time, the police had arrived. Finally, they opened the road and we drove off. I stopped the car a little distance away and we gave thanks for the Lord's protection. We were unharmed. None of us were beaten or had broken bones. How we praised Him.

Bishop Fred told us he had seen an angel sitting on the roof of the car and the angel put the men to flight. We didn't see the angel, but I know how powerful they are. The Lord said angels are "ministering spirits sent forth to minister for those who will inherit salvation" (Hebrews 1:14).

Many have testified about angels coming to their aid in times of trouble. The Bible is full of such testimonies as well. We don't pray to angels. We pray to the Commander of the angels, the Lord Jesus Christ, and trust Him for deliverance.

Be encouraged when you pray and seek the Lord for protection. He promises to deliver us from all our afflictions. Plead the blood of the Lamb and trust the Lord Jesus to help you. Focus on Him.

"May the LORD answer you in the day of trouble; May the name of the God of Jacob defend you; May He send you help from the sanctuary, and strengthen you out of Zion" (Psalm 20:1-2).

68

The Ministry of Angels

*For He shall give His angels charge over you,
To keep you in all your ways.*
Psalm 91:11

Pastor John Rose is a very dear friend of mine. I have known him and his family for over 53 years and we have kept in close touch. He is Pastor of a church in Alberton, South Africa. He has an anointed ministry to prisoners. John invited me to speak to the prisoners in the maximum-security prison just outside Johannesburg. Carl Erasmus, an anointed gospel singer, joined us.

We were assigned a security guard when we arrived. They took our watches, mobile phones, and car keys before allowing us through to the courtyard where a large marquee had been erected. I looked up at the snipers on the roof and realized these prisoners were serious, violent offenders and the wardens were prepared for any trouble.

A door opened on the left-hand side, and 1000 prisoners came hobbling in. They were shackled around their ankles and wrists. It is a very big prison, and this was just one group. Guards were positioned next to them. Some local politicians and the prison warden were seated to my left.

I shared the gospel with these men and made an altar call. "It's never too late to give your life to Jesus, "I told them. There was still no response, but I sensed the Lord moving among them. I left the podium and walked towards them. My security guard got the fright of his life and cocked his gun. The snipers stood up. Everyone froze. I was about 100 meters from them when one prisoner started shuffling towards me with his arms held up. Others followed, weeping as they came. I reckoned about 800 men gave their lives to Jesus that day.

My security guard stood very close to me. He was a high-ranking prison official and very nervous about being surrounded by people who didn't like him. I prayed with them before walking back to the podium with a relieved security guard at my side. The snipers sat down, and everyone relaxed. On our way out we passed a prison block and the prisoners shouted to me. "We could hear what you said. Don't forget us. Please pray for us."

The warden said afterwards that there was a great change among the prisoners and the wardens no longer felt threatened when they went into those blocks.

John took me aside the following week. "I have to share something with you." he said. He told me he saw two angels standing behind me and when I moved off the podium, they walked on either side of me. They were seven feet tall and carried shields and swords. An Indian Pastor was also in the marque that day. He shared with John later that he had seen the two angels standing behind me and then walking with me. It confirmed what John had experienced. Their description of the angels and their movements were the same. They are two credible witnesses.

I think we don't realise how many times angels have saved us. Perhaps you avoided a motor car accident by turning left instead of right, or hijackers fled unexpectedly. Obviously, we don't take unnecessary chances and presume that angels will rescue us. We are talking about events out of our control and in the Will of God. Do not fear, the Lord's ministering angels are watching over you.

69

The Power of the Blood of Jesus

Put on the whole armor of God, that you may be able to stand against the wiles of the devil. For we do not wrestle against flesh and blood, but against principalities, against powers, against the rulers of the darkness of this age, against spiritual hosts of wickedness in the heavenly places.
Ephesians 6:11-12

I was ministering in Zambia. Eric van Dyk was with me, and we had a good crowd on the first day. A gentleman approached me after the meeting. "Sir," he said, "My brother is demon-possessed. Can you pray for him?" "Of course," I responded.

"We will bring him tomorrow."

The next day, they arrived in their truck. "He's in the vehicle," they told me.

We walked to the vehicle but couldn't see anyone. "Where is he?" I asked.

"In the boot (trunk)."

I was startled by what I saw. The man had chains around his legs, hips, and arms. A hood was over his face."

"Is that your brother? Take the hood off him!"

"Alright," he said. "But we are not unlocking the chains. He nearly killed us last week."

They leaned him against a tree. I looked into his dark eyes. They were open, but blank.

"Demon," I commanded, you are going to leave this man's body now."

This rural African responded in perfect Oxford English. "You have no control over me. I'm not coming out. I know who you are, and you have no jurisdiction over me."

"You don't know who I am."

"I do know who you are. You are Fergus Buchan. I saw you coming on the ferry." He went on to tell me the name and address of our Mission Station in South Africa and perfectly described it. My hair stood up in the back of my head as he spoke. The meeting had started. "Take him away," I said, "and bring him back tomorrow."

The next day, we went through the same procedure. When I took the hood off, he laughed at me.

"I know who you are in the spiritual realm. You are Paul and that man with you is Peter."

"You are leaving!" I said firmly as I prayed and declared the power of the Blood of Jesus, the Lamb of God.

Nothing can stand before the Blood of Jesus. Suddenly the man's eyes opened wide as if he had just woken from a deep sleep.

"Hello, Sir," he said in his native language. "Who are you?"

"Give me the keys to those chains," I told his brothers. "The demon is gone." They were standing a safe distance away and threw them at me. I unlocked all the padlocks. Everyone looked very nervous.

"What happened, Sir?" the man said with a puzzled look on his face. He had no idea what condition he had been in. Those spiritual hosts of wickedness fled in disarray as he stood in front of the stage with his mother and two brothers, worshipping and praising the Lord with all his heart.

Are you troubled in any way today? Put on the whole armour of God, that you may be able to stand against the wiles of the devil and overcome him with the Blood of the Lamb (Revelation 12:11).

70

The Power of the Holy Spirit

And the angel answered and said to her, "The Holy Spirit will come upon you, and the power of the Highest will overshadow you."
Luke 1:35

We know that when the Holy Spirit overshadowed Mary, she was supernaturally enabled to bear the Christ-child, the Lord Jesus Christ, Son of God, Saviour and Messiah. When the Holy Spirit touches a life, powerful things happen.

We were ministering in Zambia on the copper belt. It was an open-air meeting in Ndola, one of the oldest towns in Zambia. Angus and I grew up close to that area. In those days, it was a predominantly Coloured area. The local pastors told us that the major problem in that small town was alcoholism.

As I started to preach, a large crowd arrived, including a group of very drunk people. A drunken Coloured man interrupted the meeting, and my team told him to be quiet and stand back. He was a huge man and he ranted and raved. At that point, I made an altar call.

"There's a problem in this community with alcohol," I said. "Those who have this problem, come forward and let me pray for you."

He was one of those who answered the altar call, drunk as he was. I started praying and as I said, "In the Name of..." I didn't even have time to say "Jesus" when the man fell to the floor as the Holy Spirit moved upon him. He lay there for quite a while. As we were closing the meeting, he stood up. He was completely sober and delivered instantly from alcoholic addiction. There was not even the smell of alcohol on him. He arose a new man in Christ.

"Pastor," he said, "What happened?"

"You have just been delivered from alcohol, son," I told him. "From today, you are not going to drink anymore." "Thank you," he said tearfully. "Alcohol has caused so much trouble in my life."

"Don't thank me. Thank Jesus!" I responded.

As I turned to go, he said, "I've got a question. Please tell me who punched me and knocked me out."

"No one punched you," I smiled. "That's the power of the Holy Spirit. He touched you and delivered you from your addiction."

Paul, the Apostle, saw the Holy Spirit move powerfully many times. This is his testimony: *"My speech and my preaching were not with persuasive words of human wisdom, but in demonstration of the Spirit and of power, that your faith should not be in the wisdom of men but in the power of God"* (1 Corinthians 2:4,5).

May we never hinder the powerful ministry of the Holy Spirit with human wisdom, but always be open to Him demonstrating His power as He sees fit.

71

The Pygmies and Jesus

In the same way, there is joy in the presence of God's angels when even one sinner repents.
Luke 15:10

I flew to Uganda in October 2019 where David Maindi, my friend and co-worker, was waiting. The dream and vision of reaching the largely forgotten Pygmy people was born in my heart many years ago.

We set off early for the long drive to the Congo border. Unfortunately, when we reached the border post it was closed, forcing us to spend the night in a bush guesthouse full of mosquitoes and rats. After passing through the Uganda Border post, David and I had to walk across no man's land to the Congo side where our team was waiting. Another seven hours of driving on the most atrocious roads I have ever seen brought us to Bunia, where we spent the night.

The next day we continued deeper into the Congo Basin in search of the first group of Pygmies. My heart was absolutely pounding with excitement and expectation. We had a long walk to their camp through the dense jungle and I was in absolute awe at God's unspoiled creation.

When I first laid eyes on these amazing little people my heart just melted. They had never seen a white man and my size was rather intimidating. Through an interpreter, I shared a simple message, and the response was phenomenal. Together, we knelt in the dust as they surrendered their lives to the Lord Jesus.

After that, we found another group in the jungle and their hearts were just as open to the Lord. After this amazing day, we made the long drive back to Komanda, I could hardly sleep that night as I praised the Lord for His goodness in allowing us to reach this unreached people group.

The next day we went even deeper into the Ituri forest, the remotest place I have ever been in my life. The tracker said, "Sir, pray we don't break down here!" The previous day, rebels on the run from the government ambushed and killed 18 soldiers and 10 civilians in that area. The day after we left, 100 government soldiers were attacked and killed.

After parking our cruiser, we had a 12 km walk as we searched for a third group of Pygmies. It was the thickest bush I have ever walked in. The trees towered over three stories high with a great canopy closing out much of the light.

We reached the last group late in the afternoon. Again, we rejoiced to see these wonderful people responding to the gospel. I prayed for a lady with a serious head wound from a falling tree. She had a massive fracture of the skull. The wound was packed with banana leaves. These rural people keep moving through the jungle and have no facilities. They seldom wear clothing.

Fergus ministering the Gospel to the Pygmies.

It was a long journey home. The team agreed that if even one Pygmy received the Lord, the mission would be worth it. I know the angels were rejoicing with us (Luke 15:10).

Ask the Lord to give you a passion for souls. "Those who are wise will shine as bright as the day and those who lead many to righteousness will shine like the stars forever" (Daniel 12:3).

72

The True Prosperity Gospel

So shall My word be that goes forth from My mouth; It shall not return to Me void, but it shall prosper in the thing for which I sent it.
Isaiah 55:11

We had a three-day outreach in Ndola, Zambia, where I grew up. Crowds numbering between seven to eight thousand people came to the meetings in the large football ground. We used big speakers, and the ministry reached the surrounding homes as well. The Lord prospered His Word as it went beyond the football ground.

When I am in Africa, I love to sit at the back of our truck under a tree before preaching. I don't want to be distracted so I always prefer to be quiet as I listen to the Holy Spirit for direction before ministering. As I was quietly meditating under a tree before the service, I heard a gentle voice behind me. It was a young lady.

"Good afternoon," she said. "May I speak to you, please?"

She knelt in front of me and said humbly, "Sir, I have a

gift for you." She went on to tell me she lived close by. Her husband was an unbeliever and did not allow her to listen to Christian music or preaching. "Oh," she said, "I am so blessed. Your voice came through our open window, and I heard every word. You blessed me, and now I want to bless you." The Word of God did its work without the preacher being present.

Across the field was the home of a local witch doctor. He closed his practice when he heard we were coming. He wanted nothing to do with us. He also heard the Gospel clearly every night. On the third night, he came running out of his house and onto our stage. He wept as he repented and gave his life to Christ. That man burned all his witchcraft things and the whole town heard his testimony. When they saw the power released through God's Word, the entire community was impacted, and many received the Lord as Saviour. It was an amazing experience.

Never be too cautious about sharing God's Word whenever you get the opportunity. You never know who is listening. God's Word is so powerful that it will always accomplish the task the Lord has purposed. Speak it, write it, share it, pray it. The Holy Spirit will do the rest.

73

The Universal Gospel

And He said to me, "My grace is sufficient for you, for My strength is made perfect in weakness." Therefore most gladly I will rather boast in my infirmities, that the power of Christ may rest upon me.
2 Corinthians 12:9

God's Gospel of Grace is truly universal. It reaches people and changes them, no matter who they are or where they live.

I was ministering in an area in Sudan near Juba when I had an experience I will never forget. The people in this area were Arabic. As the interpreter shared my message with them, thousands gave their lives to Christ.

"Pastor, we want to take you to the town's graveyard," one of the team said. "There are people there who need to hear about Jesus." We minister in schools, universities, and rural areas, often under trees, but this was a new experience for me.

I didn't know what to expect as we headed for the outskirts of the city. Nobody prepared me for the sight I saw. A tribe of people were living among the tombstones. Most looked like skeletons, hungry, sick, and full of sores. I have never been in an environment quite like that. As we moved among them, I could see many were dying. I was praying for people who were incontinent and suffering from diarrhoea. There was no sewage. Everything was in the open. My heart broke for them. After about three hours of ministering, I felt totally overwhelmed with what I was seeing. Everybody was crying and calling for prayer.

"Keep on going, Fergus," I sensed the Lord speaking to me. "My grace is sufficient for you."

I felt the Holy Spirit strengthening me as we continued ministering. We eventually left there in the late afternoon, rejoicing because hundreds of people gave their lives to Christ that day. I know when they pass from this life to the next, they will be in Glory with the Lord Jesus Christ.

Ten days later, I was back in London. Joanne and I set about our usual street ministry, reaching out to alcoholics, prostitutes, drug addicts, the down and outs, the homeless, and anyone we could talk to. This time we were ministering in English. We had the privilege of seeing many give their lives to Christ.

The gospel of Jesus Christ is truly universal. That's why He says, "Go into all the world and preach the gospel to every creature." It's International and everybody must hear it. So, wherever you are, whatever country you're in, whatever language you speak, keep sharing the Gospel. It is the only message that saves a lost mankind.

"For I am not ashamed of the gospel of Christ, for it is the power of God to salvation for everyone who believes, for the Jew first and also for the Greek" (Romans 1:16).

She knelt in front of me and said humbly, "Sir, I have a

74

The Widow's Mite

And He looked up and saw the rich putting their gifts into the treasury, and He saw also a certain poor widow putting in two mites. So He said, "Truly I say to you that this poor widow has put in more than all; for all these out of their abundance have put in offerings for God, but she out of her poverty put in all the livelihood that she had."
Luke 21:1-4.

I was in northern Kenya preaching at a mission station outpost. When we finished the service, the pastors put a basket on the table in front of me for the offerings. I watched an elderly widow come up to the table. She had walked all day to be at the service. That precious lady put an egg in the basket. An elderly man followed her. He put a bunch of bananas in the basket. I was very moved. That was all they had. They gave their all. My heart melted as I remembered the scripture about the widow and her two mites. It touched me deeply.

The Lord said the other worshippers gave out of their abundance. The little widow gave out of her poverty and put in all the livelihood that she had. They had plenty left over to spend on themselves. How much they gave did not interest Him. He was far more interested in how much they had left over.

Jesus said the same thing about the woman who anointed His feet with costly perfume. *"You did not anoint My head with oil, but this woman has anointed My feet with fragrant oil. Therefore I say to you, her sins, which are many, are forgiven, for she loved much. But to whom little is forgiven, the same loves little"* (Luke 7:46-47).

The pastors picked up the basket and handed it to me. There were a few shillings and some pennies nestling among the egg and bananas. We prayed and thanked the Lord for His goodness. I handed it back to them. "You keep the offering," I said. "I don't want anything."

"All right," they responded. "We will keep the money, but the egg is yours, and you can have half the bananas." They love bananas and happily divided their half among themselves.

I took the bananas and the egg and returned to my lodgings in the bush. My host boiled the egg for me, and I enjoyed it thoroughly. The bananas added the final touch to my supper. I felt so blessed.

What those two elderly believers offered to the Lord that day was all they had, but they put far more into that offering plate than all the rest combined. They gave their all. Little is much if God is in it.

75

The Wind of the Spirit

The wind blows where it wishes, and you hear the sound of it, but cannot tell where it comes from and where it goes. So is everyone who is born of the Spirit.
John 3:8

I was invited to preach in a church in Alberton, South Africa, pastored by my good friend, Pastor John Rose. The Church was full. It wasn't a healing meeting as such, but people came for prayers for healing and God graciously healed many of them.

The Holy Spirit impressed on me to pray for people to operate in the gift of speaking in tongues. I focused on that when I prayed for people who responded to the altar call. "Raise your hands," I told them. "I am praying for the Holy Spirit to move among you for the operation of the gift of speaking in tongues." Some began to pray in other tongues, but I was disappointed that there were so few. I was sure that the Holy Spirit had directed me to minister that way. We had a very blessed service, nonetheless. John and Jenny Rose, and the elders, took us to lunch and expressed their appreciation for the ministry, but I was still feeling somewhat down in my spirit.

John called me early on Monday morning. "I must share something awesome with you, Fergus. Listen to what happened on Sunday while the service was going on in the main church. There was a great move of the Spirit in the Sunday School."

He went on to share with me that there were about 150 children in the Sunday School room. Suddenly the Holy Spirit began to move there. Some of the Sunday School teachers began to weep, others were laughing in the Spirit. The children were singing, dancing, jumping for joy, and worshipping the Lord in other tongues. No adult had a hand in it. This was a sovereign move of God.

Some try to manipulate people with music, noise, emotionalism, and "the right atmosphere" and call it the move of the Spirit. God is sovereign and the Holy Spirit does not respond to human methods. We must always be led by the Spirit, and never try to lead Him to do our will.

How I rejoiced in my spirit as John shared the news. The Holy Spirit had led me to pray that prayer and His Will was done. I would have loved to have been in that Sunday School room as the Holy Spirit moved on those children.

Truly the Wind of the Spirit blows where He wishes. You hear the sound of it but cannot tell where it comes from and where it is going.

76

The Power of the Blood

And they overcame him by the blood of the Lamb and by the word of their testimony, and they did not love their lives to the death.
Revelation 12:11

Fraser and I were in the north-western area of Zimbabwe, on the Zambian border. A massive outbreak of cholera was spreading throughout the area. That is a very infectious disease and can kill you in 24 hours if you don't have the right medication. It is water-borne and the water situation in Zimbabwe was really bad. Literally, tens of thousands of people died of cholera during that epidemic.

Some pastors came to see us. "There is a massive camp set up nearby for cholera patients. There are thousands of them there in tents, but nobody wants to go and pray for them. Will you go?"

We prayed and sought the Lord. We were very aware that the situation was extremely dangerous, and we had to be sure it was the Will of God for us to go. Assured that it was, we knew the Blood of the Lamb would protect us. We broke bread, pleaded the Blood of the

Lamb over each other, and set off for the camp by faith.

John G. Lake, a healing evangelist of note, visited South Africa many years ago from the USA. He faced a similar situation. There was an outbreak of tuberculosis, also a very infectious disease, in the Johannesburg area, and he was strongly advised not to go anywhere near the area. He pleaded the Blood of Jesus over his team, and they prayed for many patients before returning to America without incident.

When we arrived at the camp, an elderly nursing sister from Zimbabwe met us. "I know you have come to pray for these people, but are you aware they have cholera?" "We are," we said. "These people desperately need prayer and that is why we are here."

We desensitised our hands and washed off our boots with disinfectant. It was a very hot day, around 40 degrees. Everywhere we looked, there were sick people. They were lying on the ground, covered with blankets. Some were burning with fever, others were shivering. Most, if not all, were incontinent. Some were semi-conscious. The stench was unbelievable.

We walked among those people for hours. Our hearts went out to them. We laid our hands on their heads and prayed. Nobody pushed us away or refused prayer. We prayed for a lot of people and led as many to the Lord as we were able. The matron thanked us afterwards. She was so moved that we had come into that dangerous situation without fear.

We are not the bravest guys in the world, but we know when the Holy Spirit is leading. If He tells us to do something, He will take care of the details. But if He does not lead us, we know not to be foolish and go into situations out of the Will of God. There is a big difference between faith and presumption. The Lord clearly said we could go in and we would be safe. And we were.

There is Power in the Blood of the Lamb.

77

Trust in the Lord

It is better to trust in the Lord than to put confidence in man. It is better to trust in the LORD than to put confidence in princes.
Psalm 118:8,9

Trust, or faith, is so vital right now because we are living in the end times. The Bible tells us things will get more difficult, the closer we come to the Rapture of the Church. This Psalm is right in the middle of the Bible, and it encourages us to trust the Lord no matter what is happening around us.

Pilots put their confidence in their planes. Commuters place their confidence in the cars or buses they travel in. We put our confidence in doctors and in lawyers. Psalm 118 says it is better to put our trust in the Lord first. If we are willing to trust a doctor, an aeroplane pilot, or a car to bring us to our desired destination, how much more willing should we be to trust in our Lord Jesus Christ to guide us? We must trust Him to look after us here on earth, to hear our prayers and answer them. *"Look at the birds of the air, for they neither sow nor reap nor gather into barns; yet your heavenly Father feeds them. Are you not of more value than they?"* (Matthew 6:26).

I've been in violent areas in Northern Kenya. I go in with my backpack and my Bible. We don't carry firearms but trust in the protection of the Blood of the Lamb. Recently we were in Northern Uganda where I spoke to a tribe that had never heard the Gospel. They still walk around with spears, bows and arrows, and practise animal sacrifice. I've been in places where they practice human sacrifice. People and princes can't help us or keep us safe, but we trust the One who can – the Lord Jesus Christ. I believe we can call upon the name of the Lord and be saved from any situation we may face.

How futile it is to trust anything or anyone more than God, especially in these perilous, desperate, evil days. We must stand together as the body of Christ and bring our praise, petitions, and pleas to the Lord.

Are you waiting for somebody to open a door for you? Or bring a solution to your problem? Search your heart today. Ask yourself: Do you trust Him more than any human being?

Repent of any unbelief in your heart right now. Make a firm decision to trust the Lord with every issue in your life and do not take things into your own hands.

"Be still and know [recognise, understand) that I am God" (Psalm 46:10 Amplified).

78

What Has God Put In Your Heart?

Then my God put it into my heart to gather the nobles, the rulers, and the people, that they might be registered by genealogy.
Nehemiah 7:5

I always had a dream of reaching the pygmy people in the Congo Basin. God put it into my heart. When a Pastor contacted me with the news that members of an unreached pygmy tribe had made contact with a local tracker, I was excited. "Are you willing to share the Gospel with them?" he enquired. It will be costly and very dangerous."

These tribes live in the Congo Basin, an area of about 2.8 million square hectares. They never stay in one place for long. Once they break camp, you may never see them again as they move further into the interior. But when God puts something into your heart, and you are willing to step out in faith, He takes care of the details.

It was a costly trip, financially and physically. First, I had to fly to Kampala, Uganda, where I met the team who were to accompany me. It was a very long drive to the border post in Northern Uganda. We walked through the border into the Congo. The heat was terrible. Our next stop was eleven hours by car, followed by another eleven-hour car trip into the interior of the Congo Forest. We parked the Land Cruisers and walked fifteen kilometres into the Congo Basin.

By the grace of God, we reached the first tribe we saw. There were about 120 pygmies camped there. I was the first white man they had ever seen. A full-grown pygmy male only reached up to my belt.

These beautiful little people listened with rapt attention as I told them about Jesus, using an interpreter. We reached three tribes in all on that trip, and many give their lives to Jesus Christ. We prayed for the sick and ministered as the Holy Spirit led. This was one of the highlights of my life as a Missionary.

"We had better leave now," the team said. "The terrorists know there is a white man in the area, and they will kidnap you for ransom or kill you."

The trip going home was just as difficult, but it was well worth the journey. I know I will see those little pygmies again in heaven because their names are written in the Lamb's Book of Life.

What has God put in your heart? Why not take some action today that will bring you one step closer to the fulfilment of your dream?

79

When You Need Wisdom, Ask God

I will instruct you and teach you in the way you should go; I will guide you with My eye.
Psalm 32:8.

Several years ago, I was ministering in Southwestern Uganda, Africa. It is a rural area, and the facilities were very basic. The mosquito net over my bed had more holes than the net! The bathroom had straw walls and one bucket.

The heat was oppressive, and I awoke early in a bath of sweat. We planned to leave that morning to share the Gospel at Lake Victoria in East Central Africa bordering Kenya, our next destination. The Pastor travelling with me looked anxious. He took my temperature. "Sir," he said, "you have been bitten by mosquitos and you have Malaria!"

There are no doctors or chemists in that area. I felt dreadful and could feel myself getting weaker by the minute. But people were expecting us at Lake Victoria, so we set off into the jungle by faith. After driving for one-and-a-half hours, I parked the Land Rover and we walked to the village. However, when we returned, we couldn't find the vehicle in the thick bush. It was stressful because we still had a long way to go and none of the three men with me could drive. How would we ever find our car?

When you need wisdom, ask God! We held hands and asked the Lord for guidance. Ten minutes later we walked into a clearing and there it was. How faithful is our God! By this time, I was beginning to see double. My head was throbbing, and everything looked hazy. We drove another ten hours to the Kenyan border. He guided us to our destination and medical assistance. If I had fainted or passed out on the way, I would not have lived to tell this story.

The next morning, we found a Clinic. A doctor was on duty, and he attended to me immediately. "You have got advanced Malaria," he informed me. He prescribed some tablets. "Take one a day, stay in bed for three days, take some painkillers, drink lots of liquid, and pray that you get through this."

"By the way," he said, "there are no chemists here so take this prescription to the hardware store where they sell chicken feed. You will get the tablets there."

By the grace of God, on the third day, my fever broke. By the fifth day, I was tweeting messages home again.

May this testimony encourage you to ask God for wisdom when you get into difficulties? Let Him instruct and teach you in the way you should go. Do not fear or be anxious.

"Your ears shall hear a word behind you, saying, *"This is the way, walk in it,' Whenever you turn to the right hand or whenever you turn to the left"* (Isaiah 30:21).

80
Whose Report Will You Believe?

*Bless the LORD, O my soul,
And forget not all His benefits:
Who forgives all your iniquities,
Who heals all your diseases.*
Psalm 103:2,3

In 1999 I was diagnosed with a very serious malignant melanoma. We were living in Germany where I was working as a Golf Professional. I planned to return to South Africa someday and go into full-time ministry, but I wasn't in a hurry. I was making a lot of money and enjoying the lifestyle. My contract was originally for two years, but eight years later we were still there.

One day Joanne noticed a pimple behind my right knee. "I don't like the look of that," she said and insisted I consult a doctor. Three days later the doctor called me. "Cancel your golf lessons. I need to talk to you urgently." The pimple was a malignant melanoma, a deadly cancerous growth. Underneath was a massive fast-growing tumour. "You have about eight months to live," he said. "We must operate right away."

I had about five operations all in all. Twice a day, they took blood tests. Eventually, the veins in my arms started collapsing. After that, they started taking blood out of my legs, and then my ankles. I was black and blue. They tested my lungs. They did CAT scans and a PET scan. The surgeons took out my lymph glands and did scans on my brain. I was reluctant to have Chemotherapy, I knew its base was mustard gas and it was deadly. They were giving it to me every second day and I reacted very badly.

I lay on my bed with an open Bible on my chest. The Word of God strengthened me. Three o'clock one morning, I called on the Lord Jesus. "I know it is Your Will that I must preach the Gospel. Forgive me for delaying fulfilling my call. If You heal me, I promise I will serve you for the rest of my life. I will resign from the golf club, go back to Africa, and go into full-time ministry."

I sensed the Presence of God. Warmth and peace came over me and I turned over and went to sleep. I knew I'd been touched by the Lord Jesus and He had healed me.

The next morning, I called Joanne. "Come and fetch me. I made a covenant with God, and I am healed. We are going back to Africa to preach the Gospel." Then I called for the ward doctor. He arrived with the oncologists and the professor in charge of my case. "I've gone to another Doctor," I told them. "His Name is Jesus Christ and He has healed me."

They insisted I have one more blood test. The following day the professor arrived with his colleagues. The Oncologist handed him my report and his face turned white. "There's no cancer in your blood," he said with a shocked look on his face.

By the Grace of God, I am still alive and preaching the Gospel in Africa, on the streets of London, and wherever the Lord sends me. The Lord Jesus Christ said, *"If you can believe, all things are possible to him who believes"* (Mark 9:23).

What is happening in your life, your home, job, relationships, or your body? Seek the Lord and spend time in His Word. The benefits of the believer include the forgiveness of our sins, and the healing of our body.

Whose report will you believe?

Now may the God of peace who brought up our Lord Jesus from the dead, that great Shepherd of the sheep, through the blood of the everlasting covenant, make you complete in every good work to do His will, working in you what is well pleasing in His sight, through Jesus Christ, to whom be glory forever and ever. Amen.

Hebrews 13:20-21

May I Pray with You?

I pray to the Lord Jesus today, asking for His grace and mercy upon you. I thank you, Lord, for every reader who has taken the time to read this book and stopped to pray. I ask Your favour, blessing, and protection on every child of Yours, in Jesus Mighty Name.

Do You Know the Lord?

*If you have never received the Lord Jesus Christ as your Personal Saviour,
please pray this prayer from your heart.*

❝ Thank you, Lord Jesus, that I can repent today of my sinful state, and for having grieved or offended the Holy Spirit. I truly repent of all my sins. I call to you as the Author and Finisher of my faith for salvation. I give my life to You today in the Name of the Father, the Son, and the Holy Spirit.
Thank You, Lord Jesus, for receiving me today. In Your Mighty Name, I say, Amen.
Please email me if you have truly prayed this prayer and surrendered your life to the Lord Jesus Christ. I would love to hear from you. ❞

Email: buchan.mmi@gmail.com

About the Author

Fergus Buchan is a missionary and evangelist. He grew up in Zambia, previously known as Rhodesia, and became a professional golfer. During his time as a golfer, he played extensively across East Africa, Zambia, and Europe. He later moved to South Africa, where he met his wife, Joanne. They moved to Germany and life was going very well for Fergus and his family. His career was flourishing, and his family was growing. They had four beautiful children – Fraser, Kirsty, Sheena, and Alastair. However, a tragic accident that took the life of little Alastair changed their lives forever. Their story is told in the book *Play It As It Lies*. The family turned to the Lord and Fergus dedicated his life to the service of God.

Fergus and Joanne have shared the gospel of Jesus Christ in many countries. His passion is Central Africa, and his heart is to reach unreached people groups with the message of Jesus Christ.

His ministry *Messiah Ministries International* is based in London, UK. When Fergus is not ministering in Africa, he walks the streets of London, seeking those in desperate need of the Lord. He also pastors a Fellowship in Fulham, London, and online via Zoom.

Fergus may be contacted at: **buchan.mmi@gmail.com**
Website: **www.mmilondon.org**

- *If you enjoyed this book, please tell your friends, and take a moment to review it online.*

More Books by Fergus Buchan

Available from Amazon
https://geni.us/play-it-as-it-lies

GOD Appointments

Fergus Buchan
with VAL WALDECK